STEPS TO INDEPENDENCE
a SKILLS TRAINING SERIES
FOR CHILDREN WITH SPECIAL NEEDS

BeHavior PROBLEMS

Bruce L. Baker
Alan J. Brightman
Louis J. Heifetz
Diane M. Murphy

ILLUSTRATIONS
BY
MICHAEL CASSARO

research press
2612 NORTH MATTIS AVENUE
CHAMPAIGN, ILLINOIS 61820

ISBN 0-87822-170-0

Supported by Contract NIH-NICHD-72-2016 from the National Institute of Child Health and Human Development: Project Officer, Michael J. Begab, Ph.D.

Dear Parent:

We are a group of professionals who spend much of our time with special children and their families. Our fields include psychology, special education, nursing, and speech and language training. We came together seven years ago, in the experience of operating Camp Freedom, a nonprofit, educational camp for children with special needs. While we watched, taught and learned from the children in this and other settings, we became involved with their parents and with the questions that troubled them. It seemed clear that parents were searching for answers—not necessarily to the complexities of retardation, and especially not in the mysterious language so characteristic of professionals. They were often simply asking: *How can I teach my child?*

We began actively to teach parents in a variety of workshop sessions focused around an educational approach called behavior modification. In a simple and direct way these workshops, over a short period of time, taught many parents to become more effective teachers. With these successes, and with funding from the National Institute of Child Health and Human Development, we set out in 1971 to develop this series of training manuals.

We called this program *Steps to Independence* (formerly the READ Project), and located it at Harvard University, under the auspices of Behavioral Education Projects, Inc. During 1972-1973, the manuals were formally evaluated with 160 families, and proved to be quite effective. Since that time, based on progressively more feedback, they have been further revised and distributed to thousands of families. This manual, together with *Early Self-Help Skills, Intermediate Self-Help Skills,* and *Advanced Self-Help Skills,* has now been published for even wider distribution.

We are continuing to revise the other READ Project manuals in the areas of toilet training, play, and speech and language; we hope to make these available in the future. In addition, we have recently completed a set of audio-visual training materials to accompany the series. We are also working on a new manual in the area of community living skills for retarded adolescents. Any inquiries concerning these projects should be addressed to us at any one of the addresses given below.

During the years that the manuals were being written and researched, a number of exceptionally talented and very committed people worked with us on the READ Project. We would like to acknowledge here the central role of Nancy B. Carroll, Benita B. Heifetz, Alexander R. James, Barbara L. Parks, John Reiser, Molly R. Schwenn and Marsha M. Seltzer. We also acknowledge the continued help and interest of Dr. Michael J. Begab, our contract Project Officer.

Over the years many parents have become our co-workers, and whatever we have been able to teach them has been repaid in kind many times over. They have repeatedly given us insights and have actively participated in the development of these training manuals. To them, also, our thanks.

Now we look forward to your joining those parents who have used these materials successfully. There is a Response Form included at the back of this manual, and we would enjoy hearing from you, too.

Sincerely,

Bruce L. Baker, Ph.D.
Alan J. Brightman, Ph.D.
Louis J. Heifetz, Ph.D.
Diane M. Murphy, R.N.

Bruce Baker is now at Department of Psychology, Franz Hall, UCLA, Los Angeles, California 90024

Alan Brightman is now at American Institutes for Research, 51 Brattle Street, Cambridge, Massachusetts 02138

Louis Heifetz is now at Department of Psychology, Yale University, New Haven, Connecticut 06520

Diane Murphy is with Behavioral Education Projects, Nichols House, Harvard University, Cambridge, Massachusetts 02138

contents

CHAPTER 1

IDENTIFY THE BeHaVIOR

Try, for just a moment, to imagine how your child experiences your world. He may see you move effortlessly through those same daily routines which are such an obstacle for him. He may hear you talking about your world and understand only bits of what you say. He may come to know that your world is a place where many demands are made on him, many skills expected, and where getting through the day is a confusing and not always a happy affair.

Your world clearly was not built with your child in mind. You are pretty comfortable in that world, knowing that whatever comes your way is more or less expected, and usually manageable. He does not see it that way. He might be more often surprised, bewildered, and incapable of managing even the most apparently simple events. In the world where you can seek and find success, he seems more often to meet with frustration and failure.

Behavior Is His Language

This manual will help you to modify your child's behavior problems. But before we begin, it is important for you to see that your child's behavior is an attempt to cope with your world and its frustrations. All of us try to arrange our world so as to avoid situations in which we may be confused, unhappy, or foolish. The special child—who meets more of these situations than we do—tries to arrange his world likewise. Often he cannot talk fluently enough to tell us how he is feeling or what he would like changed. Behavior, in many cases, is the special child's language, his loudest voice.

Through his behavior your child can tell you things about your world that he might not otherwise be able to say. And so, if you are to be successful in managing your child's problems, you must learn to listen to the language of his behavior. Listen, for example, to how his behavior might say: (a) "That's too difficult for me," (b) "I'm tired now," (c) "Why won't you play with me?" or even (d) "I love you." And, too, you must learn to respond to his behavior in a language he can understand. That's what this manual is all about.

Changing a child's problem behaviors is far from simple. Perhaps, like many parents, you've tried before, met with mixed results, and now feel unsure about trying all over again. Nevertheless, a new commitment to reducing your child's problem behaviors can prove as rewarding for you as it has for the many other parents who are now using this manual's approach effectively at home. It wasn't easy; this manual is long and requires active involvement. But they have succeeded in reducing their children's behavior problems—and you can, too.

The manual is written to be adapted and used in ways that you determine make sense for your child. We do not pretend to offer specific solutions for each and every problem situation; it would be impossible. We do, however, intend to offer you our general approach for looking at and eliminating behavior problems so that you can have some guidelines for helping your child. This is possible.

What Is a Problem Behavior?

Your first task will be to decide exactly what is a problem behavior for your child. In the end, *you* must be the judge.

It may be that your child has obvious behavior problems, such as hitting, or screaming or running away. It may be that he bites his hands or scratches himself. Behaviors such as these are relatively easily defined as problems. On the other hand, your child may exhibit behaviors which pose problems in a more subtle way—crying when you leave him, wandering aimlessly, or rocking back and forth for hours.

It is often inappropriate behaviors such as these, rather than limited learning abilities, which lead others to view a special child as different and to react to him differently. At home, these behaviors further limit a child's opportunities to learn and they are a disruption to the household. In our experience, three types of behaviors are called problems:

Behaviors which interfere with learning

Eileen screams and hits whenever her parents try to teach her to identify pictures.

Eileen's acting up in teaching sessions is most apt to occur when she is asked to do something new. Her behavior makes it very difficult for her parents to work with her and, as a result, slows down her learning. "Acting-out" of this sort is one way a child's behavior says "No" to a learning situation, and the result is often that adults quit trying to teach.

Mike spends much of his time rocking from side to side.

Mike's rocking isolates him from other people and from materials in his world. By being absorbed in this behavior, he misses many opportunities to learn and do things throughout the day. Behaviors which limit a child's growth are not all of the dramatic, temper-tantrum variety; the child who rocks or wanders aimlessly, or sits absorbed with an object for long periods misses a great deal also.

Behaviors which interfere with skills already learned

Polly's mother has to stand over her and constantly urge her to dress herself.

Polly has learned to dress herself completely, but her stalling forces others to do things for her which she *can* and *should*

3

be doing on her own. Polly enjoys the attention she gets this way and her mother becomes especially annoyed; she knows Polly can dress herself.

Alison freezes at the top of a stairway, refusing to walk down alone.

If someone tries to get Alison to walk downstairs by herself, she pulls back, turns pale and screams; someone always ends up carrying her down.

Alison has a special type of problem behavior: she is afraid. Since a fall on the stairs many months ago, she has been terrified of walking down stairs, even though she is quite able to do this by herself.

Many children have fears like this; some children are afraid of water, or dogs, or darkness. Fears limit the opportunities a child has to learn new skills or to practice those already learned.

Behaviors which are disruptive to the family or harmful to the child

Jackie cries and screams every night at bedtime.

Jackie's crying and screaming at bedtime are very upsetting to the rest of her family. The other children are kept awake, and her parents have to spend much of their evening sitting up with her. It has reached the point where everyone dreads the bedtime struggle.

Behavior problems often lead families to make many adjustments from the way they would like to live.

4

Mark has temper tantrums; he screams and bites his hand.

Mark's self-abusive hand biting is especially upsetting to his family and dangerous to him. Hand biting is certainly painful and might well lead to permanent damage. More than almost any other behavior, self-abusive behavior is difficult to understand and upsetting to see.

Behavior is a powerful language indeed for a special child. And, as you can see from these examples, a great variety of behaviors can be problematic, because they:

1. Interfere with learning

2. Interfere with skills already learned

3. Are disruptive to the family or harmful to the child

Actually, most behavior problems fall into more than one of these categories. For example, Alison's fear of stairs both disrupts the family and prevents her from practicing a skill she has already learned.

No doubt you have read the above examples with your own child in mind, and it is likely you see his problems as fitting into one or more of these categories. We'll return to your child's behavior problems shortly. First, however, we want to introduce you to an essential aspect of the behavior modification approach—looking beyond the behavior to the context in which it takes place.

The A-B-C Pattern

Behavior does not occur in a vacuum. Acceptable behaviors *and* problem behaviors both take place in an identifiable context. Consider a simple example:

"He kissed her."

A simple description of behavior usually leaves us with questions like: "When?" "Where?" "And then what happened?" To really understand behavior, we must look beyond just the act itself to the conditions surrounding its occurrence.

The *setting* in which the behavior occurs (When? Where?) helps us to see if the behavior is appropriate. For example, "He kissed her" will be interpreted quite differently depending on whether he did so "... on her doorstep" or "... at the office."

What *follows* the behavior helps us to predict if it will happen again. "He kissed her on her doorstep" might be followed by:

"She slapped him" or "She asked him to come in."

We know much more about "the kiss" when we view it in this broader and more specific context. The setting, together with what took place before the kiss (Antecedents), and with what followed it (Consequences), are both necessary to understand the behavior fully.

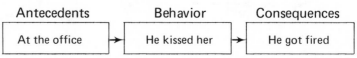

Antecedents	Behavior	Consequences
At the office	He kissed her	He got fired

Had the antecedents been different, the behavior might not have been inappropriate—and it might have brought better consequences.

Once we can describe both the setting in which a behavior occurs (Antecedents), and the actions which usually follow the behavior in that setting (Consequences), we are better able to predict whether the behavior will continue there or not. A simple rule to remember regarding the consequences of behavior is the following:

Behaviors followed by pleasant consequences are more likely to happen again.

For example:

Antecedents	Behavior	Consequences	Future?
On her doorstep	He kissed her	She asked him to come in	More likely to happen again
On her doorstep	He kissed her	She slapped him	Less likely to happen again

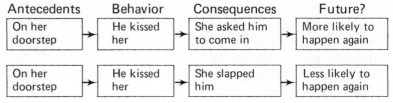

A knowledge of Antecedents and Consequences and their combined effects upon behavior allows us to manage behavior in a systematic and successful way. This is the central theme of behavior modification, and we shall be returning to it often as we examine the variety of ways you can put it into practice for behavior problem management.

Before going into the details of how you can reduce your own child's behavior problems, we want you to see an overview of the behavior modification approach. Therefore, the next several pages will relate the story of one child, Gary, and how his family set out to modify his troublesome mealtime behavior. This simplified account is based on an actual case, as reported by his parents. The "Gary story" will give a further illustration of the A-B-C notion, and will give you an introduction to other ideas which we will develop in the remainder of this manual.

Gary's mother began:

Gary's Story

"Gary's really driving us crazy at mealtimes. Every few minutes he jumps up from his seat and ducks under the table, or wanders around the kitchen, opening drawers and emptying them

out. If we insist that he stay in his seat, he'll scream and cry. Either way, the meal is hectic. . . ."

To get a more exact picture of Gary's problem, we asked the family to keep a record of his behavior. For one week—while reacting to him as they always had—they were to note how much time went by after the start of each meal before Gary jumped up.

At the end of a week their record looked like the chart on the following page.

How much time until Gary jumps up

	Sun.	Mon.	Tues.	Wed.	Thurs.	Fri.	Sat.	Average
Breakfast	18 min	15 min	10 min	13 min	12 min	14 min	16 min	14 min.
Lunch	19 min	15 min	11 min	13 min	16 min	16 min	15 min	15 min.
Dinner	3 min	2 min	5 min	7 min	3 min	4 min	4 min	4 min.

Gary's mother talked about the record:

"It was a pretty typical week. I was surprised, though, how much sooner he gets up during dinner than during breakfast and lunch. I guess I'd never noticed how big the difference is; he almost always stays seated until he's through at breakfast and lunch. When thinking about this, it dawned on me that at dinner my husband is home and we're likely to be talking—or trying to talk—at the table. At breakfast and lunch Gary gets more of my attention. You know, I noticed that Joe and I are usually in the middle of a conversation when Gary jumps up."

Gary's behavior problem occurred when the family's attention was not directed to him. In other words, the antecedents of the behavior were *dinnertime,* when Gary *did not receive attention.*

She continued:

"When he gets up, of course, we have to get up too, run after him, and bring him back to the table. He would miss most of his meal if we didn't, and he would probably destroy the kitchen in the process."

The consequence of Gary's behavior problem was attention from the family.

"During the week we got the whole family together and talked about what we would do. My daughter suggested that we pay more attention to Gary at dinner since he usually stayed in his seat when someone was paying attention to him, so we agreed to do this. At the same time, we decided to ignore him when he got up. This way, he would get attention only at the table, and might decide to stay there. I wasn't too sure I liked the idea since he might not come back at all, but my husband pointed out that he wouldn't go hungry for too long and would be all the more ready for the next meal. We rearranged some drawers in the kitchen so that he would not destroy too much, and we decided to try the ignoring approach."

The family was instructed to continue keeping records, but just for the dinner meal since the problem more often occurred there. At first Gary got up very soon and stayed away the entire meal, trying to get the family's attention. After a few days, however, he began to stay at the table longer and come back on his own after just a few minutes.

"At first I thought we'd never live through it. When he would be emptying drawers or tugging at my sleeve, it was not very easy to ignore him, but the whole family was great at helping each other. As soon as Gary sat down again, everyone leaped in to talk to him and give him loads of attention.

The records showed that the length of time Gary sat at the table before he got up was increasing. During the first week of this program the average at dinner was 5 minutes. By the next week he was spending most of the meal at the table (13 minutes). By the following week Gary sat 16 minutes, which was the length of the entire meal; he would only get up then if dessert was delayed. We decided to put Gary's progress on a graph on the wall for everyone to see.

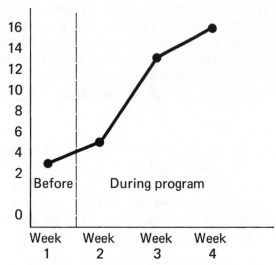

Average minutes before Gary gets up

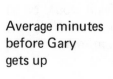

"We all decided we would reward ourselves for helping Gary to make such progress by going to a restaurant for dinner—and now we could even take Gary along."

No two children are alike. Each has his own way of doing some things, not doing others, and acting with his own unique style in both. No example we might offer, therefore, could ever make you say, "Yes, that's my child all right!" For even when your child's inappropriate behaviors are similar to Gary's or others' we shall describe, they will always be just a little different, too. Yet there are common ways to look at, understand and change all problem behaviors, no matter how unique your child seems to be.

Let's briefly note some of the things which Gary's family had to do.

Examine the behavior

1. *Specify the behavior exactly.* Gary's mother did not talk in general terms. She did not say that Gary was "hyperactive" or had "horrible table manners." Rather, she very specifically outlined what Gary did: "He jumps up from his seat, and runs around the kitchen."

2. *Take a "before" measure.* Likewise, she did not say that he jumps up from the table "very soon" or "right away." Rather, she timed how long Gary sat at the table each meal, and wrote down the times. This "before" measure was to prove helpful in starting a program.

3. *Identify the A-B-C pattern.* The family discovered that Gary's problem occurred at dinner, when their attention was not directed towards him. They also noticed what followed his behavior: their attention! By looking beyond the behavior itself to what came before and what followed, his parents began to get some ideas for changing that behavior.

Initiate a program

1. *Change consequences*

   a. Remove positive consequences from the problem behavior. The family decided that when Gary started his usual behavior of jumping up, they would ignore him. Soon Gary found that jumping up provided little attention.

   b. Provide positive consequences for an alternative behavior. When Gary was sitting in his seat, or when he returned to the table, he was given considerable attention. Hence, Gary could only receive attention when he was sitting in his seat.

2. *Change antecedents.* Gary's family also made some changes in the dinner arrangements so that Gary would be less likely to leave the table. He was brought to the table just as the food was being served, he was seated in a corner, and he was given attention during the meal.

3. *Continue to measure the behavior.* By continuing to keep track of how long Gary sat, his family could compare his behavior after the program was initiated with the "before" measure, and could thus determine the effectiveness of the procedures.

In summary, Gary's family followed 6 steps in planning and carrying out a program to modify his problem behavior.

They examined the behavior:

1. Specified the behavior exactly

2. Took a before measure

3. Identified the A-B-C pattern

They initiated a program:

1. Changed consequences

2. Changed antecedents

3. Continued to measure behavior

This manual will consider each of these six steps in more detail.

Now that you have seen, in general, how we will approach a behavior problem, it's time to begin a program for your child.

1. Get a pencil.

2. Read the rest of this manual in the order presented; do not skip around as you might do with a magazine. Also, plan to read the entire manual before beginning a program.

3. If possible, have other family members read the manual also, and talk about each section with them after everyone has read it.

Take a Break!

CHAPTER 2

examine THE BeHavior

Close your eyes for a minute, and picture a child who is hyper-active. Really. Put the manual down for just a moment and imagine. . . .

Imagine a hyperactive child.

What did you picture the child doing? Was she running around in circles? Climbing up the bookshelves? Bouncing up and down on the sofa? Banging a spoon on the plate? Chasing the cat?

Specify the Behavior

Perhaps you imagined none of these. Perhaps you pictured them all—and more! In any case, we can be sure you didn't imagine a child sleeping or sitting quietly, so the term hyperactive at least narrowed the range of behaviors you might think of. But it did not tell you *exactly* what the child *does.*

To change behavior, you must be able to specify exactly what the child does. General terms like hyperactive, aggressive, stubborn, immature or lazy may be helpful for general conversation, but they do not pinpoint exactly which behaviors are a problem. A more exact description of behavior is needed.

Note how Gary's mother described his problem as "jumps up from his seat and ducks under the table." This is a more useful description than calling Gary "hyperactive," if we are to actually change his behavior. A good description should give something specific *to see* and *measure.*

The following example shows the importance of *specifying the behavior exactly.*

example

Mary Clarke was a new salesgirl in a big downtown department store. When describing Mary, a co-worker said, "She's a good worker, but she has a poor attitude."

Suppose, just for a moment, that you were Mary's supervisor. How might you go about improving Mary's attitude? You might lecture her; you could praise her on those days when her attitude is better; you could threaten to fire her; you could send her a written warning. But about what? You would have to communicate to her *exactly which behaviors you are concerned about and how you want those behaviors to change.*

Mary's "poor attitude" could be almost anything, such as:

Coming late to work
Sleeping during staff meetings
Getting upset when a customer doesn't buy something
Being impolite when a customer asks for help
Bringing her St. Bernard to work with her

Therefore, when a co-worker says Mary has a "poor attitude," you, as her supervisor, would need to get a more exact description in order to decide whether the behavior should be changed and, if so, how. Each of the behaviors listed might be approached in a different way and some, in fact, might not be viewed as a problem at all by the supervisor.

14

In order to reduce your child's behavior problems it is important, just as it was with Mary, to know *exactly which behaviors* you want to change. Here are several behavior problems, first with a too general description and then with an *exact description.* Note that only the *exact description* enables you to know which behaviors to work on.

General Description	Exact Description
Gary is "hyperactive."	Gary jumps up from the table at dinnertime.
Eileen has "temper tantrums."	Eileen screams and hits when she is in a teaching session.
Polly's "lazy."	Polly takes over one and a half hours to dress in the morning if she does not receive help.
Mike is "in his own world."	Mike sits in a chair and rocks from side to side.

Which of the following descriptions *specify the behavior exactly?*

> Joan kicks the cat.
> Tim's always getting into trouble.
> Charlie is just plain lazy.
> Rosalie keeps opening the refrigerator.
> Sally throws food.
> John is selfish and spoiled.

If you chose the girls, you're on the right track! Their problems are described specifically enough to be seen and measured. On the other hand, Tim's "trouble," for example, could be many things: hitting other children, shoplifting, swearing, and so on.

Now think about your child's behavior problems—*in specific terms.* Write on the lines below several of the problem behaviors which you would like to modify.

_____

_____

_____

_____

_____

If you wrote a specific description, you are ready to think about measuring behavior.

Wait A Minute. Did you actually write down the behavior problem? Is it described as specifically as possible? If so, good. You deserve a break before reading further.

If not, please do.

We have found that parents who write in the manual are far more successful in reducing behavior problems than those who just read through it.

Measure the Behavior

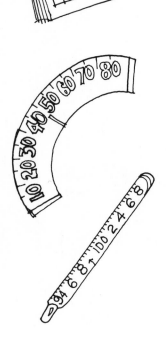

Once you have defined a problem in terms of specific behaviors, you are ready to measure how often these behaviors occur. We learn little by hearing that Gary jumps up from the table "soon after" dinner begins, or that Mike has tantrums "often." We learn more by hearing that Gary only stays at the table for an average of 4 minutes or that Mike has 2 tantrums each day. Unless we can describe the occurrence of Gary's and Mike's behavior problems in numbers, we cannot see if their behavior is changing over a period of time. If you rely only on words to describe behaviors, you will never know if what you've modified is more than your vocabulary!

To be sure, record-keeping may not be the most natural thing for you to do. Yet, for at least two reasons, keeping track of what you observe is essential to the successful management of behavior problems. *First,* without accurate records it is sometimes difficult to know if a program is really working. Our memories tend to be faulty, and it's often unclear to us whether a child's behavior problem has decreased or not. Records make this clear and show us when it is wise to change our teaching approach. *Second,* you will need some encouragement yourself, and records of your child's progress can be rewarding for you. They will show you beyond a doubt that your efforts are paying off—and that's nice to know.

Although the thought of record-keeping makes many people nervous, just think how much you already use numbers throughout the day. You can count, and you can tell time—so you already have all the skills you will need for record-keeping!

Ways to record behavior

In many cases, keeping track simply means counting *how many times* the behavior happens or, in other words, its frequency of occurrence. For example:

Mark had two temper tantrums (screams, kicks, bites his hand) today.

Larry tears his clothes an average of 7 times a day.

Bobby hit another child 11 times during recess.

In other cases, keeping track requires clocking *how long* the behavior continues each time it occurs—its *duration.* For example:

Polly takes an average of 90 minutes to dress in the morning.

Jill played with the puzzle for 45 seconds before wandering off.

Jackie continued to cry for 25 minutes after being put to bed.

You will record either the *frequency* (how many times it occurs) or the *duration* (how long it lasts) of the behavior problem. In our case example, Gary's parents recorded the duration of time he stayed at the table before getting up the first time.

To decide whether you should count the frequency or clock the duration of a behavior problem, ask the following question: "Will counting *how many* show me if I'm reaching my goal?"

Counting "how many times" Polly gets dressed in the morning certainly will not provide that information because the goal in this case is to reduce the *length of time* it takes her to dress. On the other hand, counting how many times Mark has a tantrum (screams, bites hand) each day would answer the question because the goal is to decrease the *number* of tantrums.

Think about the following behavior problems and decide whether counting "how many" or "timing how long" would be best.

Joan kicks the cat.
Tim cries every night before going to sleep.
Charlie does his chores slowly.
Rosalie keeps opening the refrigerator.
Sally throws food.
John rocks back and forth.

These are not easy at first. If you decided *to count how many for the girls* and *time how long for the boys,* you score 100%.

Joan kicks the cat.	*Count how many.* The goal is for Joan to kick the cat fewer times or not at all.
Tim cries every night before going to sleep.	*Time how long.* Counting the number of nights Tim cries will not give enough information; we already know that he cries every night. You want to reduce the length of crying time.
Charlie does his chores slowly.	*Time how long.* Charlie already does his chores, but the goal is for him to do them faster.
Rosalie keeps opening the refrigerator.	*Count how many.* It doesn't matter if it takes Rosalie 2 seconds or 2 hours to open the refrigerator. The goal is to decrease the number of times she does it.
Sally throws food.	*Count how many.* Again, we want to reduce the number of times Sally throws food; how long it takes her to do it is unimportant.
John rocks back and forth.	*Time how long.* To count the number of times John rocks, even for a short period, would require too much effort. A duration measure of how long he rocks is better.

Before measure

Your first record-keeping will be a *before measure*—recording your child's behavior for one week *before* you begin a specific program to change it.

We've all seen ads in the back of magazines for miraculous new exercise programs guaranteed to give anyone a perfect figure or physique. In order to convince you to sign up for their program, they show a *before* and *after* picture. The *before* might be a 300-pound woman, compared to the same woman *after* at 110 pounds. The numbers and pictures are there as proof that the exercise program really works.

This is exactly what we are asking you to do with your child—to get a *before* and an *after* picture of his behavior in order to judge whether your approach has been successful, or whether the program should be changed.

In our account of Gary's behavior problem, his family kept a *before* record for one week; at every meal they wrote down how long Gary remained seated after everyone sat down. During this week they did not change their usual way of reacting to Gary. This record-keeping was easy, it required very little extra effort from the family, and it gave them a good record of his behavior problem. You will remember that at the end of the first week their chart for dinner looked like this:

Time in Minutes

Dinner	Sun.	Mon.	Tues.	Wed.	Thurs.	Fri.	Sat.	Average
	3	2	5	7	3	4	4	4

When you begin to take your before measure, you might find that it is difficult to decide at times whether the problem has occurred. It may be that you will still have to define the problem more specifically.

If more than one member of the family is helping with record-keeping, you should talk about what you each consider to be the problem. Remember, you will be measuring either frequency (how many) or duration (how long). Gary's family measured duration.

Will counting "how many" show me if I'm reaching my goal?

"Yes"—Count how many
"No"—Time how long

The following is an example of specifying a behavior and taking a *Before Measure*—in this case, frequency.

example Here we go again! Betty was in tears, the castle she had so carefully built was in shambles, and John was "in trouble," about to get his usual scolding. But first, Mrs. O'Neil put another check on the chart. She was taking a before measure of John's problem behavior, which she had once called "not playing nicely." After thinking about his behavior more exactly, she had re-named the problem "interfering with toys while Betty is using them." During this *before week* she had been instructed to respond to John's "interference" as she always had, with one exception: She was to note on a chart each time this behavior occurred and then she could get on with the usual scolding. Yesterday the total on the chart was only one, but today it was already three.

In this example, Mrs. O'Neil recorded *every time* John interfered with Betty's play. It was easy to count because it happened infrequently, about 3 times a day. Therefore, it was possible to record *every time* the problem occurred. With infrequent behaviors, whether you are recording *how many* or *how long,* you should record every time the behavior occurs.

Other relatively distinctive and infrequent behavior problems for which you could obtain a complete record over the entire day might include any of the following:

running away
violent outbursts of temper
breaking furniture
tearing clothes
fighting
hitting someone
screaming

Many behavior problems occur so frequently, however, that you could not get a complete day's record: You would have to follow your child all day to record the problem, and would have little time to do anything else. For these more frequent problems, you will only record at specific times during the day.

Some problems occur *only* at a particular time or in a specific situation, for example, at mealtime, or at bedtime, or during a bath. For these, the observation time is pretty obvious. For other problems, which occur at a variety of times during the day, you will need to decide on a specific observation time (or times). Use the following guidelines:

1. Select a time (usually 15 to 30 minutes is long enough) when the behavior is most likely to occur, and keep track of the behavior when it occurs during this period.

2. As closely as possible, observe during the same time period (or periods) each day.

You might choose to observe for several 20-minute intervals, or for the first 5 minutes of every hour, or for the hour immediately following dinner, or. . . whatever. The exact time is up to you, as long as it is a time when the behavior is likely to occur, a time which is convenient for you, and as close as possible to the same time each day. The main point is to be *consistent* in your measuring; make sure that you measure only for the specified times.

When is a behavior frequent enough to record only at certain times?

A rough guideline is: If the behavior occurs more often than once in 15 minutes, record only at specified times. If it occurs less frequently, record every time it occurs throughout the day.

Bobby would very frequently hit, or push, or kick his brothers. Now Bobby's teacher has begun to report this same behavior toward other children at school. It clearly seemed time for the family to do something about it. They decided that a good time to observe would be from 6:00 to 6:30 in the evening, just after dinner and when the boys were usually engaged in play. During this 30 minutes Dad recorded—by putting an X on a chart—every time Bobby hit, kicked or pushed one of his brothers. At the end of the 30 minutes Dad totaled the Xs. Below is his record for a two-week *before* period.

example

Chart

WEEK (Write in Date)	Days							Average for Week
	S	M	T	W	T	F	S	
Week 1 3/21– 3/27	xx xx **4**	xxx xx xxx **8**	xxx xx x **6**	xxx x x **4**	xxx **3**	Noˣ home	xxx xx **5**	5
Week 2 3/28– 4/3	xxx xxx x **7**	xx xx **4**	xxx xx x **6**	xx xxx **5**	xxx xxx x **7**	xx x **3**	xxxx xx xx **8**	6

Before

21

A wrist counter or a supermarket hand adder is a very convenient—and very accurate—way to keep track. A piece of masking tape on your wrist makes a convenient substitute for paper, too, and gives you a permanent record of the day's activities which you can stick into a notebook. For timing, you can use a wristwatch, wall clock or even a stopwatch, if you have one.

On the first day Bobby hit, kicked, or pushed 4 times, on the next day 8 times, and so forth. His dad figured an average for each week—but we'll talk more about that later. For now. . . .

Do not go on until you have completed this page.

Record-Keeping Summary

What to observe:

1. Select a behavior problem.

2. Specify the behavior exactly, so that the members of your family can agree about whether the behavior has occurred or not.

Write the problem behavior here: _____

_____

How to observe:

1. Decide whether to count *how many* or time *how long* (or both).

   Ask the question: Will counting "how many" show me if I'm reaching my goal?

Write whether you will measure how many or how long here:

_____

When to observe:

1. If the behavior is infrequent, observe all day.

2. If the behavior is frequent, or occurs only in a certain situation, observe for a shorter time period.

Write whether you will observe all day or for a shorter time period here: _____

If a specific time period, when will it be?_____

When you have completed page 22, you are ready to begin taking a one-week measure of your child's behavior. Fill in the record chart below, and begin to record your child's behavior tomorrow. Continue to make your record until you have finished reading this manual and are ready to begin to modify the problem. This should be at least one week.

Which exact behavior are you observing? _____

BEHAVIOR CHART

When are you observing it? _____all day _____minutes per day   from_____ to _____

Are you charting _____ how often it occurs?

or _____ how long it lasts?

Week Write in Date	Days							Average
	S	M	T	W	T	F	S	
Week 1								
Week 2								
Week 3								
Week 4								
Week 5								

Identify the A-B-C Pattern

GET THE WHOLE FAMILY INVOLVED

We have already introduced the A-B-C notion (Remember the kiss?). Once you have *specified* a behavior problem exactly and have begun to take a *before measure* of it, you will want to identify the A-B-C pattern in order to initiate a program.

Remember Gary's example:

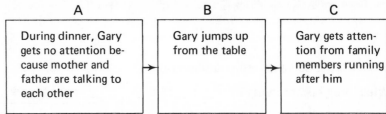

A	B	C
During dinner, Gary gets no attention because mother and father are talking to each other	Gary jumps up from the table	Gary gets attention from family members running after him

This diagram makes clear how important it is to view Gary's behavior in its context. A behavior problem should not be seen as just the child's problem alone, but rather as a give and take between the child and his environment. When viewed in such a context, "problem behaviors" are successful ways the child has of getting what he desires from his environment. And, remember, you and the other members of your family are the most important parts of his environment.

What has Gary learned? He's discovered that a good way to get attention at dinner is to jump up from the table! Furthermore, every time this A-B-C pattern is repeated, Gary learns his "behavior problem" even better. The next time he wants attention at mealtime, he is more likely to use the method which has worked best in the past—that is, to jump up. Gary's behavior problem, it turns out, is not a problem to him at all. It's a solution for getting attention. Remember the rule we mentioned earlier:

Behaviors followed by pleasant consequences are more likely to happen again.

Remember to see the A-B-C pattern from your child's point of view. You may not feel that chasing, scolding and the like are pleasant consequences. Yet to a child, all of these forms of attention may, in some way, be "pleasant." You'll know if the consequences you provide are rewarding by seeing whether or not the behaviors they follow happen more or less frequently in the future.

Remember, too, what Gary's family discovered: *Their* behavior formed the Antecedents and Consequences of Gary's problem behavior. Once they recognized this key point, they were able to alter their own behavior so that Gary was no longer reinforced for leaving his seat.

When thinking about the antecedents and consequences of your child's behavior problem, take an especially close look at how your own behavior fits in.

Another example will show the importance of discovering the A-B-C pattern.

Jackie's family sees *crying* as her behavior problem and begins to look more carefully at its antecedents and consequences. A closer look reveals that it occurs most predictably at two times during the day. First, she cries in the afternoon when her mother tries to hold a short speech teaching session. Her crying is so disturbing that her mother soon quits teaching. The A-B-C pattern seems to be:

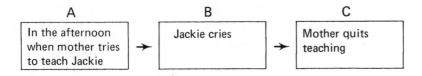

A   B   C

| In the afternoon when mother tries to teach Jackie | → | Jackie cries | → | Mother quits teaching |

Also, every night it's the same story. Jackie is all smiles until it's bedtime, and then the tears begin. They last, in fact, until mother gives in and lets Jackie come downstairs again. The A-B-C pattern here is:

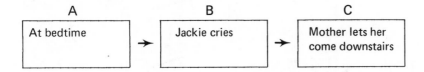

A   B   C

| At bedtime | → | Jackie cries | → | Mother lets her come downstairs |

Note that the behavior in each diagram is the same: "Jackie cries." In the teaching session, this behavior makes a difficult task "go away." At bedtime the same behavior now *brings* attention from the family along with other benefits, such as TV.

Only by seeing that there are different contexts (A-B-C patterns) to Jackie's behavior are we able to see that different approaches will be necessary.

In the teaching instance, Jackie's mother might simplify the speech task so that Jackie can do it easily, and then continue to teach right through the crying, having a reward ready for success. At bedtime, Jackie's family might change the consequences by ignoring Jackie's tears. Depending on the context, then, a behavior might be dealt with in many different ways.

We have talked about specifying the problem behavior, taking a before measure and determining its A-B-C pattern. We're now ready to talk about initiating a program—changing antecedents and consequences to reduce the problem behavior and to increase more appropriate behaviors.

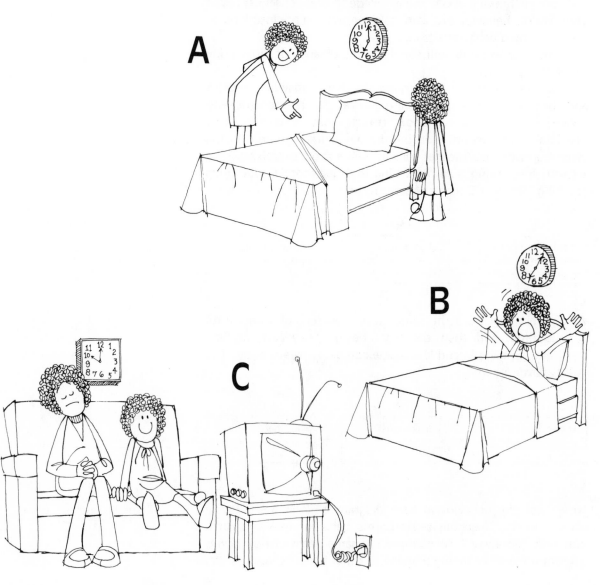

CHAPTER 3

INITIATE a Program

Identifying the A-B-C patterns of a problem behavior may be something of an "eye-opener" for you: It is for many parents. Indeed, your child's behavior does not occur because of some mysterious condition. It happens, instead, because easily observable Antecedents and Consequences act to guide and encourage what your child—and all of us—do every day.

In this section, then, we will look in more detail at one part of the A-B-C pattern, the Consequences, to determine what events in your child's world may be maintaining his problem behavior and how you can change them. Then we shall examine the Antecedents in the same way.

All of us are concerned with the consequences of what we do. We quite naturally tend to do what *pays off* for us in one way or another—for example, in money (paychecks), the approval of others (praise, a smile), the promise of good things to come (vacations), or the pleasant, private feeling of a job well done. Likewise, we tend *not* to do what might bring about unpleasant, painful or fearful results. When was the last time, for example, that you wanted to put your hand on a hot radiator, or looked forward to denting your front fender?

Your child's behavior is motivated in the same way. He, too, has learned to behave according to expected consequences, to do what is likely to lead to events which are rewarding for him. Likewise, he has learned to avoid behaving in ways that would bring unpleasant, nonrewarding events. Simply stated, then, we might describe both his and your behavior in any given situation by our familiar rule—and by its opposite:

Behaviors followed by pleasant consequences are more likely to happen again.

Behaviors which are *not* followed by pleasant consequences are less likely to happen again.

Change the Consequences

27

To review Gary's case for a minute, *attention* was a pleasant consequence. According to the first rule, since his behavior of jumping up from the table was immediately followed by attention from the rest of the family, it is safe to say that Gary's mealtime behavior problem would likely continue.

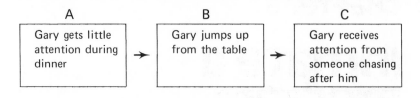

A	B	C
Gary gets little attention during dinner	Gary jumps up from the table	Gary receives attention from someone chasing after him

Carefully observe what usually happens to your child immediately after his problem behavior. In what ways do you or other family members respond to him that might be rewarding and, therefore, encourage his actions to continue?

Based on our experiences, we can identify three general kinds of consequences which often reward problem behavior. Hopefully, the job of locating the particular ones which are motivating your child's behavior problems will be a bit easier after you become familiar with these examples.

Attention

Children, all children, continually seek attention. The child who works hard in school, or helps Mom with the dishes, or shares his toys does so, at least in part, because of the positive attention these behaviors bring from others. It comes as no surprise that hugs, smiles, interest, and praise are rewarding and therefore encourage much "good" behavior. What might come as a surprise, however, is that *the consequence that most frequently maintains problem behaviors is also attention.*

We are not referring simply to a sitting-and-looking kind of attention, but to any one of a wide variety of ways a child can get a response from others—some not usually recognized as rewarding. We all know that praise, smiles and hugs are attention, but the attention that follows behavior problems might take other forms, including coaxing, chasing, scolding, frowning, arguing, lecturing or even simply making eye contact. Each of these, in one way or another, says to the child, "Because of what you did I am reacting to you." And although some of these kinds of attention seem to us not as pleasant as a hug or a smile, the child with limited ways to get "nicer" attention often must settle for these.

Take Polly. Although she knows how to dress herself, she stalls and refuses, creating a problem in the morning.

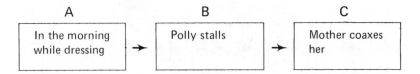

A   B   C

A	B	C
In the morning while dressing →	Polly stalls →	Mother coaxes her

It is clear, when we examine the A-B-C's of this situation, that Polly has learned a successful strategy for getting mother to pay attention to her. Isn't it likely, therefore, that as long as mother continues to coax, Polly will continue to stall?

Activities

When an infant cries, we automatically assume he is hungry or in some other way uncomfortable. He wants something and, oftentimes, plain old attention doesn't seem to fill the bill entirely. So we feed him. Or, when he's a bit older, we invent games that capture his attention. And when presented with these activities, his crying usually stops.

Since infants do not remain infants for too long, we do not worry about encouraging crying behavior by these activity rewards. As an infant develops, he can either make his needs known verbally (without crying), or he can satisfy them himself by getting his own food, playing his own game, or whatever. And he can wait awhile, if necessary, for his needs to be satisfied. For some children, however, the ability to say, or do, or wait, develops more slowly and often to a more limited degree. For these children, needs and desires might be expressed most easily in the language of behavior. Parents of these children sometimes encourage behavior problems unknowingly by continuing to reward them with activities.

The parent, for example, who has discovered that three cookies will usually end her daughter's tantrum behavior doesn't realize what the daughter is learning: That to get the cookies all she has to do is scream and kick. Activities, then, like eating, playing games, going for a ride in the car or for a walk outside—these, too, are effective consequences that are often found to be maintaining problem behaviors.

Activities which *increase problem behavior* might either be given to a child if he acts up enough, or promised to him if he will become quiet. For example, note the following two common reactions to behavior problems which can serve unintentionally to maintain them.

"Oh, let him watch the television. I can't stand to hear him scream about it any more."

Once you have said *no* to something, it's very difficult to "stick to your guns" with your child screaming, kicking, running

around the house or perhaps just looking hurt or unhappy. And, surprisingly, as you give in to him and let him have or do what he wished, you find it seems to work—he becomes quiet and happier! For this reason, many families fall into a trap of giving in to—and thereby rewarding—their child's problem behaviors. The immediate result is that the behaviors diminish, and that is rewarding *to you.* But the long-range result should be obvious by now: your child has learned that the next time he wants his way, his problem behavior should certainly work.

"If you stop that crying right now, I'll give you a piece of cake."

Often parents will try to "make a deal" with their child *during* her behavior problem. Think for a moment what this child has learned about behaviors which will bring her something nice—like cake! In order to be rewarded for stopping, she must first start. So, if the usual family response to problem behavior is one of "rewarding it away" for the present, isn't it only natural that this behavior will continue to occur in the future?

Escaping or avoiding

Sometimes we find ourselves in situations so uncomfortable that all we can think of is "How can I get out?" That situation may be a crowded bus, a boring conversation, or a visit from Uncle Jack's 10 children and his German Shepherd dogs. Whatever it is, the most rewarding consequence in such situations is to be away from them—to be rid of those circumstances we find so uncomfortable.

Think now of children who are being asked to learn—whether in school or at home—and who are not experiencing much success. It is not unusual to see a child at school deliberately misbehave, knowing that the teacher will probably send him out of the room for awhile. His acting may in this way be encouraged by the teacher, if the consequence is to escape the discomfort of a difficult lesson. Furthermore, the next time the child sees the lesson coming he may not even wait to be in it, but might begin misbehaving early enough *to avoid* the certain frustration altogether.

A good deal of problem behavior at home is rewarded by this kind of escape/avoidance payoff. Most often, such consequences will be specific to certain situations involving (1) new demands, such as teaching situations where he is being asked to perform new skills; or (2) activities that the child just doesn't like, such as bath time or bedtime. Many children soon discover that some well-timed crying and a nicely performed tantrum will get them "off the hook," or even postpone the event altogether.

As we said earlier, behavior is often the child's most effective language, and in this language it is easy to see how many different kinds of problem behaviors are saying "Let me out" or "I want to be somewhere else." Many a child has stayed up a little later or gone to bed without a bath because Mom or Dad couldn't put up with the problem behavior. The child's avoiding strategy, in other words, has won out. Many children have literally cried a teaching session to a screeching halt—and in so doing learned a successful escape strategy.

Remember Eileen?

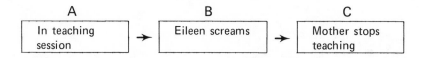

| A | B | C |
| In teaching session | Eileen screams | Mother stops teaching |

Eileen's escape from the teaching session is obviously pleasant to her. But by ending the teaching session when she did, what behavior has Eileen's mother strengthened? When we allow the child to escape or avoid certain situations because of such behavior, then certainly we are encouraging its recurrence.

Think more about your child's behavior problems. What events usually follow immediately after them? Do you scold, coax or comfort him in an attempt to quiet him? Do you bargain with him, promising something pleasant if he stops? Do you give in (or give up) when his problem behavior clearly says, "I want out"? On the next page write down the consequences you've located for your child.

Behavior Problem   Rewarding Consequence(s)

_____   _____

_____   _____

_____   _____

_____   _____

Note: There are some behavior problems which do not seem to fit the A-B-C pattern because we cannot readily identify what Consequences in the child's world are maintaining the behavior. The two main types of behaviors which do not obviously fit the A-B-C model are fearful and self-stimulating or self-injurious behaviors. For example:

Alison's freezing at the top of the stairs

Mike's rocking

Chapter 4 discusses these behaviors and how to deal with them. Please read the rest of the manual first, however, before turning to it.

Locating a Better Consequence

Once behaviors are understood in terms of the consequences they present to the child, strategies for reducing problem behaviors become a little more obvious. In order to change a behavior, you must change those consequences that have been maintaining it. This may involve either not paying off the child with pleasant consequences (no rewards), or paying him off instead with unpleasant consequences (punishments). Our preference—here and always—is to focus as much as possible on the no-reward consequence rather than the punishment consequence.

Ignoring

Rearranging the consequences of a behavior problem so that attention or activity rewards do not follow is more commonly known as *ignoring*. Ignoring means *not* coaxing, *not* chasing, *not* scolding, *not* giving an activity, *not* looking—almost *not* noticing. It is a sure way of letting the child know that *no reward* will follow his problem behavior.

Ignoring is the easiest consequence to describe, yet one of the most difficult to do effectively. In a way, it is an unnatural response on your part. And often it is just plain uncomfortable. But, too, it is one of the most successful ways found by parents to reduce behavior problems.

Your child almost always wants your attention. What you are teaching him when you ignore him during specific problem behaviors is that there are certain ways he will never get it. In other words, if he wants a pleasant consequence to his behavior, then that behavior had better be something other than a problem. In Gary's story, you'll remember that once the family identified their attention as the rewarding consequence, they decided to ignore Gary when he was out of his seat.

Now let's look at another example on the following page.

example

Almost every morning when her brothers and sisters left for school, Roberta had a temper tantrum: She pounded her fists, pulled at the drapes, and cried. Her mother would try to calm her down by singing a song to her or by playing with her. Sometimes this worked and Roberta would eventually stop; the next morning, however, she would start right in again.

It is not hard to see that Roberta gets a reward—her mother's attention—each time she has a tantrum. Because her tantrum behavior is rewarded, it is likely to happen again and again.

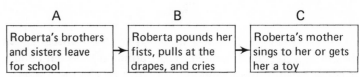

A	B	C
Roberta's brothers and sisters leave for school	Roberta pounds her fists, pulls at the drapes, and cries	Roberta's mother sings to her or gets her a toy

Roberta's temper tantrums will continue as long as mother continues to reward them.

In this case, a logical rearrangement of the consequence should change Roberta's well established—and very common—behavior problem. Instead of paying off the tantrum behavior with rewarding consequences, Roberta's mother would be wiser to ignore it, causing a new pattern to look like the following:

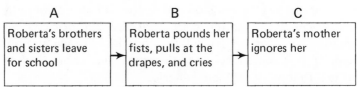

A	B	C
Roberta's brothers and sisters leave for school	Roberta pounds her fists, pulls at the drapes, and cries	Roberta's mother ignores her

Roberta's temper tantrums will soon decrease as long as mother continues to ignore them.

Of course, it is important to ignore only those problem behaviors which will not be harmful to your child. Roberta's mother, for example, knew that Roberta wouldn't really hurt herself seriously (and the drapes were strong enough!) so she could safely ignore that behavior. If, however, Roberta's major problem was one of continually running into the street, then another strategy for changing the behavior would have to be chosen. We will consider such alternative strategies in a moment.

First, though, let's briefly consider two questions frequently raised about ignoring:

Is there a best way to ignore?

Often, when a problem behavior such as screaming, or jumping up and down is "driving me crazy," ignoring seems like the most impossible thing to do. At such times, the best way to ignore is to leave the situation, go to another room, turn on the radio, pick up a magazine or whatever. In other words, distract yourself away from the problem behavior so that you do not risk attending to it by accident. At other times your child may be seeking attention by interrupting conversations, climbing up on your lap, pulling on your clothes, and the like. It is much harder to leave these situations, and there's no real reason why you should. Instead, look away, continue talking, and firmly remove him from your lap, but say little to him (other than "I'm busy now").

There is really no one best way to ignore and, like most parents, you will undoubtedly develop your own most effective style. If you keep in mind why you are ignoring, then your behavior should follow correctly enough: You're ignoring so as not to reward problem behavior with your attention. You're not going to look at it, yell at it, argue with it, or in any way let your child see that you even recognize it. In this way, your message to the child is clear: This problem behavior isn't going to work any more! It will no longer be successful for you and a problem for me!

What will my child do when I ignore?

As far as your child is concerned, his problem behavior has always worked before—in fact, that's how he learned to get your attention whenever he wanted it in the first place. What, now, when suddenly things change? When the old tricks fail?

For most children the response to your new reaction is predictable—they will try even harder to get your attention. We might imagine a child, for example, being actively ignored for the first time saying to himself: "I don't get it. Am I yelling loud enough? Mom always used to try and calm me down by now. Maybe I better add a little crying or kicking; something that'll get her over here."

That's right. In all probability, you can expect your child's problem behavior to get a little worse before getting a lot better because your new reaction to it requires a little testing on his part before it's to be accepted. So here, in the beginning, is where you have to be the strongest: To continue ignoring even when it seems that his behavior is getting worse instead of better. It won't be that way for very long.

Removing the reward

Just as you moved yourself and your attention away from the problem behaviors, you can remove activity rewards as well. Both strategies ensure that problem behaviors will not be followed by pleasant consequences.

Often a certain situation will make it easier and more effective to simply take the reward away from the child. The following are examples of such situations:

Taking away Kelly's plate for one minute when she plays with her food.

Shutting the television off until Pete stops whining and sits quietly.

Taking the ball away from Fred for two minutes when he deliberately throws it at the cat.

When using this type of consequence, you must always provide a ready way for the child to get back what you've taken away. That is, in most cases you will remove the reward for a brief period of time and then give it back, as in the following example.

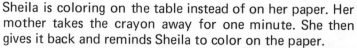

example Sheila is coloring on the table instead of on her paper. Her mother takes the crayon away for one minute. She then gives it back and reminds Sheila to color on the paper.

If, indeed, the crayon is rewarding to Sheila, then her mother's strategy should discourage further coloring on the table. Perhaps it may have to be repeated several times and with continued reminders, but eventually Sheila will learn that the only way she can keep the crayon is by coloring on the paper. If this strategy fails after several times, and if Sheila can understand the rule, then her mother should simply say something like the following:

"If you color on the paper, then you may keep the crayons for the rest of the afternoon. If you color on the table, then I'm going to take them away for the rest of the afternoon."

She must, of course, keep her word, and Sheila might well have to wait until evening before getting her crayons back. At this time, if she is really looking forward to coloring, she will be much less apt to do so on the table.

What happens, though, if Sheila, angry at her mother for disrupting her play, starts to cry or rip up the paper? In this case she would be wise to ignore the outburst as we discussed earlier and return the materials to Sheila only after an agreed upon time—and only if she is quiet. Mother's patience and her understanding of the strategy will combine to eventually decrease Sheila's behavior problem.

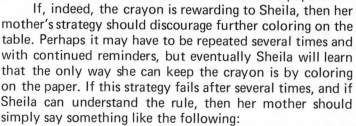

Time out

When a behavior problem is so disruptive that ignoring proves too difficult or ineffective and there is nothing rewarding to remove, then a Time Out strategy should be used. Time Out means putting the child in a situation where any possibility for reward is removed entirely for a fixed period of time, usually not longer than 2 to 5 minutes. For example:

Sitting on a chair in the corner for two minutes.

Sitting on the floor away from the family for three minutes.

Sitting in the hall alone for five minutes.

Staying in a room alone for five minutes.

Notice that in each of these different situations the length of time is always short and should be specified in advance. The child is simply, and without undue attention, removed from the place where the behavior problem occurred to another non-rewarding setting.

It is common for parents to send a child to his room or make him sit in a corner when he misbehaves. We may resort to such strategies when we are angry, perhaps, or when we just don't know what else to do. We want the problem to go away, literally, and it does. *This, however, is not Time Out,* and there is little reason to expect that the troublesome behaviors removed in this way won't return again soon.

Time Out is not a response made in anger or on the spur of the moment. It is, instead, a strategy decided upon in advance for dealing with one carefully specified behavior. Going to Time Out should never be a surprise for any child.

Time Out is also a procedure that requires careful thought while being carried out. Like ignoring, it is much easier to describe than to do.

Also, Time Out does not mean being locked up. It does not necessarily mean leaving the area where the behavior problem occurred. Remember, simply defined, this strategy refers to *Time Out from an opportunity to receive positive rewards.* So, if a problem behavior occurs which you cannot successfully ignore (e.g., the behavior may be dangerous to your child or to others, the behavior may be attracting rewards more powerful than your attention), then you might well decide to take your child away from the source of his reinforcers for a short period of time. This is what we mean by Time Out.

example

The O'Connors had started a program of giving Jimmy a 3-minute Time Out (alone in his room) whenever he spit at someone. This was an unpleasant situation for him.

One day, Jimmy and his two older sisters were playing catch. Jimmy missed the ball and spit at one of the girls. She immediately whisked him off to his room, being careful to give him as little attention as possible. When the 3 minutes were up, she went to bring Jim out of his room—but as soon as she opened the door, he spit at her again. If she had then let him come out to rejoin the game, she would be following his last behavior (spitting) with a reward (ending the Time Out). This is exactly what she didn't want to do.

She told him, "No spitting; you stay here for another 2 minutes!" She tried not to give him too much attention, but at the same time made sure he understood why he had to stay. When she came to get him the next time and he didn't spit, she brought him out to play again. Mrs. O'Connor made a special effort soon after that to praise Jimmy for playing nicely with his sisters.

In the next few pages we will suggest guidelines for how to use Time Out in the home. Read them through carefully and discuss them with family members who might be involved. If, after no more than 2 weeks, you find that the problem behavior is pretty much unchanged, you should re-examine what you're doing. Is everyone responding to the behavior in the same way? Is your child discovering ways to make the Time Out procedure rewarding? Is he receiving plenty of attention when he's not misbehaving?

Guidelines for time out

1. Specify in advance the behavior for which your child will be in Time Out. This reminder need not be made frequently, but rather at those times when it's likely that the problem behavior will occur. Your explanation should be brief, clear and to the point, and it should communicate to your child:

   a. A precise picture of the behavior (in words he can understand).

   b. The location for Time Out in your house (a certain chair, a particular place).

   c. How long Time Out will last (never more than 5 minutes, usually around 2).

2. Once you're sure your child knows what not to do, you don't need to say very much when he does it—and you shouldn't. This is not the time for apologies or debates. It is the time to act firmly on what you have already said:

"When you spit at someone, you go to Time Out."

There is no more information you can add at this point, so don't. Ignore the crying, the "I'm sorry," the "I won't do it again." These are all predictable responses to being put in Time Out; no child, after all, should want to go willingly.

3. "Go to Time Out." These words alone will rarely get your child on his way, and will probably have to be accompanied by some guiding on your part. Take hold of your child's wrist firmly, not aggressively, and walk him silently to the Time Out area. Again, ignore whatever tantrum behavior he may start. Look straight ahead. Remember, this Time Out strategy is a new one for him, and the fact that you are really following through with it may be the newest and most upsetting part of all. This, however, is what makes it effective.

4. The first few times after you bring your child to the Time Out area, it is unlikely that he'll sit there nicely for the 2 to 5 minute period. He might scream; he might kick; he might look for something to throw (of course, if you have left something within arm's reach of the Time Out space, then you have simply invited this last behavior). As long as your child remains sitting, however, he should be allowed to do any of these—and to learn that you won't respond with even a glance. If he gets up, however, then you must respond.

Physically return him to the Time Out area—firmly again, but matter-of-factly—and "stand guard" nearby, giving him no attention whatsoever. You may well have to repeat this procedure several times, but if you perform consistently enough, remaining as calm as you can throughout, this will quickly stop being fun for your child, and he should soon learn to "stay put."

5. Have a kitchen timer nearby, and set it for 2 to 5 minutes when the Time Out period begins. Your child will soon learn that his actions during Time Out can have no effect on the timer and, by always setting it this way, you'll be sure to remember when the Time Out period ends. Kitchen timers have helped more than one parent to ignore appropriately and to be consistent with the Time Out procedure.

6. Not all children will rush from the Time Out area as soon as you tell them the period is over. Some may be holding a grudge and will not want to do anything you say. Others may still be crying. In any case, once the Time Out period is over,

they should leave, and this exit may again require your physical assistance. Remember, your child was put in for one, and only one, specific behavior. It is up to you to show him that you can ignore the others. If he wants to hold a grudge for now, that's fine. It won't last long. Neither will the problem behavior for which he was put in Time Out.

7. Though the exit from Time Out should not be accompanied by attention (a simple, "You can come back now," will do), you should look quickly for behaviors to reward when your child returns to his previous situation. Even if he decides to hold a grudge a bit longer, now is the time for you to emphasize the kinds of behaviors that will always get your approval and attention.

So far you haven't mentioned anything about punishment as a way to control behavior problems. I've always found that a well-placed spanking now and then can prove quite effective. Am I wrong?

No, you're not wrong. Like yourself, many parents have found that a well-timed spanking—now and then—can put a quick end to certain very annoying or dangerous problem behaviors. We have simply not included this physical punishment strategy in our discussions because we want you to develop a *systematic approach* to behavior problem management. Systematic means planned, not impulsive; it refers to consistency rather than "now and then"; and it implies long-term rather than temporary solutions.

No doubt an occasional slap on the wrist might appear effective, but if our concern is to develop a consistent approach instead of a hasty reaction to behavior problems, we would always prefer to use one of the other procedures described.

First, when you hit or spank a child, you are very clearly demonstrating a form of behavior he is likely to imitate. And, while we can never know exactly where a child first picks up this aggressive behavior, it is likely that your reacting to him this way might encourage it further.

Secondly, the parent who easily or inconsistently resorts to physical punishment might come to be looked upon by the child as dangerous or frightening. Effectively teaching your child—or simply enjoying the day with him—will certainly be less possible if he is continually on the lookout for a spanking.

Finally, as we noted earlier, what you may think of as traditional punishments may be seen by your child as a unique form of attention, and then act in just the opposite way that you intended, thus maintaining rather than decreasing the problem behavior. To be slapped or spanked has, for some children, the same effect as to be scolded or chased; we know this simply because, for these children, punishments act only to stop the behavior at the moment while doing little to prevent its occurring again. Relative to the other strategies we have discussed, in fact, you teach your child very little through physical punishment—and there's little pleasant about having to do it anyway. So, for your sake and for your child's, avoid the use of physical punishment whenever you can think of an alternative strategy.

You can no doubt see by now that what we have been calling problem behaviors are really, from your child's point of view, successful or rewarding behaviors. They are not "bad" or "troublesome" as far as he is concerned; to the contrary, they work well to get him what he's after. He has learned that they pay off.

Encouraging Alternative Behavior

Now suddenly the payoff is removed. A behavior that might have been scolded before is ignored; when he might have been chased before, he's now put in Time Out. You are beginning a strategy to reduce problem behavior. But your child doesn't know that! All he sees is that those behaviors which used to be successful are now met with a different, nonrewarding consequence. And, as a result, he will soon be left to search for new ways to get your attention.

Here is where you can be his most effective guide. This is your chance to step in and teach him appropriate, nonproblem behaviors that will now work better to get him what he wants and make life a lot more pleasant for the entire family.

Now is the time to point out clearly to your child—both in what you say and by what you do—the variety of alternative behaviors that will be followed by a pleasant, rewarding consequence.

If we look in once again on Gary's family, we will see that changing the consequences of his problem behavior (ignoring him when he was out of his seat) was only part of their approach. His family also decided to pay special attention to him when he was sitting at the table—to talk to him more often, to comment on his manners, and, in general, to include him in more of the mealtime activity. They were extremely careful not to let Gary's desirable "sitting" behavior go unrewarded.

Thus, Gary was still able to get—and his family was still able to give—all the attention he wanted. But he had to learn that at mealtimes the only place he would get it was at the table. If you are to change problem behavior successfully, then you, too, must show your child which desirable behaviors will be rewarded. It sounds simple enough, we know, but keep in mind that we all sometimes tend to "leave well enough alone." And, as in Gary's case, when this happens too often, children quickly look for ways of behaving that are difficult to ignore.

Your search for desirable behaviors to reward will be much more successful if you can think of ones which are *incompatible* with the problem behavior. A behavior is incompatible with problem behavior when both cannot happen at the same time.

For Gary, running around the room and sitting at the table were incompatible. If the "sitting" behavior becomes strengthened, the "running" behavior must become weakened.

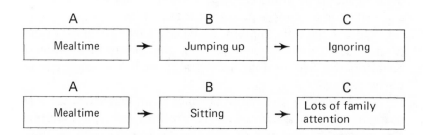

A		B		C
Mealtime	→	Jumping up	→	Ignoring

A		B		C
Mealtime	→	Sitting	→	Lots of family attention

These two A-B-C patterns must exist together if Gary's behavior problem is to be effectively reduced.

Two part strategy:

Undesirable Behavior—Remove Rewards
Desirable Behavior—Give Rewards

The "solutions" we have suggested thus far, then, are only "half-solutions." Take Roberta, for example. When her brothers and sisters leave for school, she pounds her fists, pulls at the drapes and cries. While at first Roberta may have been genuinely upset, we saw that her mother reinforced this behavior with attention and a toy. Therefore, it had become a predictable routine.

Our suggestion that mother begin to ignore Roberta during this "tantrum," however, is only part of the program. Her mother should also be rewarding incompatible behaviors. *She should be ready with attention and a toy immediately when Roberta is not crying and away from the drapes, perhaps playing quietly or talking.* There should always be two A-B-C diagrams.

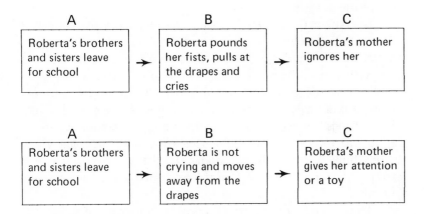

A	B	C
Roberta's brothers and sisters leave for school	Roberta pounds her fists, pulls at the drapes and cries	Roberta's mother ignores her

A	B	C
Roberta's brothers and sisters leave for school	Roberta is not crying and moves away from the drapes	Roberta's mother gives her attention or a toy

Roberta now has a choice and, according to our rules, she will become progressively less likely to "tantrum" (which brings *no* payoff) and more likely to be occupied in some other way (which brings a definite payoff).

Similarly, remember Sheila? Her coloring on the table was to result in the crayons being taken away. Yet the incompatible behavior of coloring *on the paper* should be rewarded with attention, praise, perhaps another crayon. Mother should look in periodically, prepared both to (1) remove crayons for coloring on the table and (2) praise for coloring on the paper.

"Good Sheila, you've been coloring on the paper. That's nice."
"Dad, see how nicely Sheila is coloring on the paper."

Every program has these two parts: discouraging the problem behavior and encouraging alternative behaviors.

Decide for your child's problem behavior an alternative, incompatible behavior which you can encourage. Write it below:

_____

_____

TAKE A BREAK

Change the Antecedents

So far we have talked primarily about changing the consequences of problem behaviors. In many ways we are talking as though you must be constantly on guard for one of two things to happen—something troublesome which you must then decide to ignore, Time Out, or whatever; or something appropriate which you must then quickly reward. It's not easy, though, being always on the lookout, being the one who always has to react. And, in fact, it's not entirely necessary.

Essentially, we have only considered the B-C part of the A-B-C pattern. The likelihood of problem behaviors can also be changed by paying close attention to the Antecedents, the A-B part of the pattern.

By Antecedents, you'll recall, we mean the situation just before the problem behavior occurred. Some Antecedents almost seem to guide the child to act in a troublesome way. As you well know, there are certain times and places where your child's behavior problems are most likely to occur. For example, a child might be more apt to cry when he's tired, to get "into things" when he's being ignored, to scream when he cannot do the task, or to fight over a toy with his sister when there's only one toy in the room. The list of situations which can point a child toward problem behaviors is a long one indeed.

The following section will consider a variety of ways you can arrange your child's world so that it encourages appropriate behavior.

Teach your child new skills

In addition to encouraging specific alternative behaviors which are incompatible with the problem behavior, you can, and should, teach him a variety of new behaviors as well. We have written a number of manuals about skill-teaching, and feel that it is important to be always engaged in skill-teaching as well as behavior problem management. A day filled with skills, after all, has less time left for problem behaviors.

Gary's parents, for example, while continuing to ignore his "jumping up" behavior, might also have taught him some new mealtime skills, like cutting with a knife, pouring, or serving.

Joe's parents might teach him more play activities with his toys, so he would be less inclined to throw them.

And as Polly's parents help her to polish up her dressing skills so that they become more routine for her, she may stall less.

The child who has a greater variety of behaviors to choose from in a situation is less likely to choose a problem behavior.

Reward your other children as examples

Show your child what behaviors you would like from him (and show him that these will pay off!) by rewarding your other children for these behaviors. This can be a planned strategy with the entire family helping. Other children can demonstrate the appropriate behavior, and your rewarding can be done in an exaggerated and obvious way. It can also just be done naturally.

When Joe is throwing toys: "Debby, that's really good. I like how you're playing with your toys."

When Polly dawdles while dressing: "Sally is all dressed—and see how nice she looks."

When Mark refuses to wash his hands: "Come and look, Dad, at how nicely Jimmy is washing *his* hands.

This "rewarding others" strategy is a good one when you want to ignore your child's problem behavior and at the same time encourage an alternative behavior. Ignore him—and praise someone else!

Set the stage so behavior problems arise less in teaching sessions

Even though you attempt to teach your child new skills and show him what is expected, behavior problems will nevertheless still arise while you try to teach. Often ignoring or Time Out will not be effective since the child is, in fact, not seeking attention but trying to avoid an unpleasant task. You can help him behave appropriately by making certain that you have given him tasks appropriate to his current skill level, and by being alert to cues that the task must be simplified (such as eyes wandering, squirming in the seat, whining, and so forth).

Our manuals on skill-teaching have stressed *setting the stage for success*—essentially arranging the antecedents so that your child will find tasks easy for him, so that he can readily succeed. We have discussed gearing demands to a child's level of functioning and increasing them gradually, by small steps. We have talked also of choosing easy-to-manage materials, giving understandable directions, eliminating distractions, and so forth. All of these are examples of arranging the Antecedents—or *setting the stage*—in an attempt to encourage appropriate behavior and make problems less likely to occur.

Let's return for a moment to two children who should be familiar to you by now. Notice that as well as rearranging consequences (so the problem behavior no longer pays off) their mothers also encouraged alternative behaviors.

Eileen's mother scheduled a very short teaching session and kept the demands very simple. She continued to teach in spite of any screaming. *She rewarded Eileen immediately for sitting quietly and paying attention.*

Arranging the Antecedents.

Encouraging alternative behavior.

Polly's mother laid out Polly's clothes so that she could easily put them on. She then paid no attention whatsoever to Polly except when Polly was dressing herself. *At these times, her mother praised her and told her how nice she looked.*

Arranging the Antecedents.

Encouraging alternative behavior.

And finally, Gary. If his family had moved the table next to the wall and sat Gary at one end, they would have instantly reduced the number of directions he could run off to. Also, by waiting to bring Gary to the table just as dinner was being served, they would have certainly reduced the likelihood of his becoming bored and jumping up.

Set the stage so behavior problems arise less throughout the day

There are countless times throughout the day when changing the situation just a little reduces the likelihood of problem behaviors: Simply giving your child something enjoyable to do, removing breakable objects, providing an extra toy, stepping in to help for a moment. . . .

Think for a moment about your daily routine. No doubt you have already made some adaptations to help your child get through the day more smoothly. Perhaps you eat earlier because that's when he gets hungry. Or you've lowered the toothbrush holder so that he can reach it. Or you cut his meat for him before you sit down to eat. There are countless ways in which you might already have changed antecedents to make problem behaviors less likely.

Two cautions

1. Make certain that you do not change antecedents so much that other aspects of your family life become entirely disrupted. Cooking *only* your child's favorite food may keep him at the table, as would talking constantly to him and only him; but mealtime for the family would then become an ordeal. Take the whole family into consideration when rearranging antecedents and, if the change must be an uncomfortable one, it should be short-lived as you gradually phase conditions back to normal.

2. Make certain that you do not change antecedents so that not only problem behavior but almost all other behavior as well is prevented from occurring. Gary, for example, could have easily been prevented from running away from the table at mealtimes by being tied to his chair. A child who hits other neighborhood children could be prevented from doing so by keeping him in the house—or even placing him residentially in a distant community! Then, too, highway accidents could be prevented by banning the automobile! The obvious difficulty in each of these examples is that they maneuver around the behavior problem rather than dealing with it directly. Hence, if Gary is untied or the other child returns to the neighborhood, nothing has been learned.

In sum, change antecedents only enough to reduce the likelihood of the behavior problem occurring, remembering that you are changing your child's world in order to teach him something. Your own world should not be turned upside down in the process.

Actually, your home (the way it's arranged, the events which happen) provides situation after situation which we could accurately describe as "teaching sessions" for your child. Some last no longer than perhaps 30 seconds ("Tommy, would you please put this spoon away in the drawer"); others may continue quite a bit longer ("When you've finished cleaning your room, then you can watch TV"). Some you may structure very carefully ("This is a spoon, Tommy, and this is a fork. Now point to the spoon"); others may just happen ("If you keep playing with the dial like that, I'm going to turn the TV off for good").

Once you recognize the many opportunities for learning which continue throughout your child's day, you are in a position to develop these into mini-teaching sessions. These sessions will in turn limit the occurrence of behavior problems by communicating clearly to the child what is expected and, of course, what is rewarded during them.

Structuring your child's day more intentionally can help motivate him to perform skills he already has. Consider, for example, the morning routine: Getting up, washing face, brushing teeth, combing hair, getting dressed, making the bed, coming to the kitchen for breakfast. . . . If your child can already do some of these skills, a wall chart may be very helpful. You can award checks for completing tasks. You might require that he have a certain number of checks before he can come to breakfast; or that he complete the tasks in a certain amount of time if he wants breakfast.

Checks for breakfast? Sure. Breakfast is usually an effective reward when someone hasn't eaten for an entire night, so why not arrange the antecedents of the morning routine in such a way that in order to get breakfast the child has to come to the kitchen with a certain number of checks on his chart. You might simplify matters by rewarding tickets (small pieces of paper which you and he have made up) if he has a certain number of checks. He would need, say, one ticket which could be earned by getting 3 checks in order to get a basic breakfast. A second ticket—earned by doing all the tasks—could help him gain "extras," a donut, more juice, raisins on his cereal. If successful in completing his tasks, he'll be able to hand the tickets proudly to you for breakfast and your enthusiastic praise.

No matter how you decide to structure the way rewards are given for the morning routine, the most important aspect of your teaching will be approaching the management of behavior problems both positively and preventively. Keep in mind, also, that what works for the morning routine will work as well for other situations across the day: Bedtime, after school, going shopping, visiting neighbors.

Thus far we have talked about keeping records of your child's problem behavior for a week or so *before* initiating a program. An important part of the program will be to continue record-keeping *after* you begin the program as well. These *after* records will be extremely useful when deciding whether or not the program is working.

Take your *after* measure beginning with the first day of the program, and in the same way as you took the *before* measure (during the same time every day). Bobby's father (in our example on page 21) kept these *before* records:

Continue to Measure Behavior

Week (Write in date)	Days							Average
	S	M	T	W	T	F	S	
Week 1 3/21 – 3/27	X X XX 4	XXX XX XXX 8	XXX XX X 6	XXX X 4	XXX 3	Not home	XXX XX 5	5
Week 2 3/28 – 4/3	X XX XXX X 7	XX XX 4	XXX XX X 6	XX XXX 5	XXX XXX X 7	XX X 3	XXXX XX XX 8	6

His *after* records looked like this:

Week 3	XXX XXX XX 8	XXX XXX XXX 9	XXX XXX XX 8	XXX XXX 6	XXX X 4	XXX 3	XXX X 4	6
Week 4	Not home	XXX XX 5	XX 2	X 1	XX 2	XXX 3	XXX 3	3
Week 5	X 1	0	XX 2	XX 2	0	Not home	X 1	1

What if I miss a day's observations. Doesn't that throw the total off?

Yes, it does, for then the total would be only based on 6 days instead of 7—and would not be comparable to other weeks. A way to avoid this problem is to find the *average* for each week: Divide the total for that week by the number of days you *actually* observed. This will show you what happened on a typical day.

For Bobby, the weekly averages for hitting, kicking or pushing looked like this:

BEFORE start of program   week 1   Average=5 per day
    week 2   Average=6 per day

AFTER start of program   week 3   Average=6 per day
    week 4   Average=3 per day
    week 5   Average=1 per day

An average makes week-by-week comparisons easier to understand. As you can see, by the third week of the program Bobby's problem behavior was greatly reduced.

As you begin a program and are continuing to record your child's behavior, there are several cautions we should mention.

1. *The problem behavior may get worse before it begins to get better.* Your child's behavior problem, as we have seen, may be maintained by attention, by a favorite activity, or by escaping from an undesired task. When the behavior fails to bring these expected consequences, the natural tendency for him will be to try a little harder—to cry louder and longer, to hit again to see if you're looking. Stay with the program at this early and critical time and expect that very soon you'll see a change for the better.

2. *Again, stay with the program.* It is tempting to begin a program, continue it for a few days, and then decide that it's "not working" and needs change. A new program is then begun, perhaps for a week—and so on. Given that problem behaviors have been learned over weeks or months or even years, it is certainly unreasonable to expect that a program will eliminate them "instantly." Devise a program which makes sense to you, and then stay with it for several weeks. Give it a chance to work.

At the end of the manual there is a blank Behavior Chart. You should use it to record your *before* and *after* observations. On page 51 is the Behavior Chart as it was completed by Bobby's father.

What do I do about the graph *on the behavior chart?*

We have included a graph for those parents who would also like to see their progress in this form. Actually, graphs make your records easier to read and your progress more notable. Let's briefly consider how to use the graph.

What exact behavior are you observing? _Hit, Kick or push his brothers_

When are you observing it? _____ all day. __30__ minutes per day, from __6:00__ to __6:30__

Are you charting __✓__ how often it occurs or _____ how long it lasts?

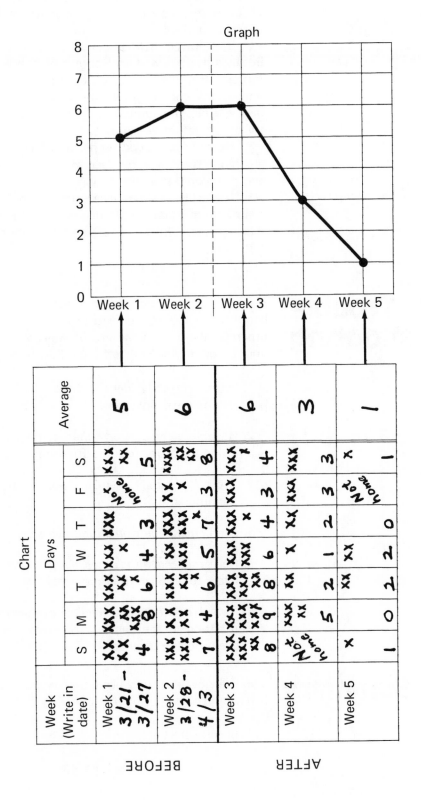

Chart

Week (Write in date)	S	M	T	W	T	F	S	Average
Week 1 3/21 – 3/27	xx xx 4	xxx xxx 8	xxx xx 6	xxx x 4	xxx 3	Not home	xxx xx 5	5
Week 2 3/28 – 4/3	xxx xxx 7	xxx xxx 4	xxx xxx 6	xxx xxx 5	xxx xxx 7	xxx xx 3	xxx xx 8	6
Week 3	xxx xxx 8	xxx xxx 9	xxx xxx 8	xxx xxx 9	xxx x 4	xxx 3	xxx x 4	6
Week 4	x 1	xxx xx 5	xx 2	x 1	xx 2	3	xxx 3	3
Week 5	1	0	2	2	0	Not home	x 1	1

BEFORE / AFTER

The Behavior Chart shows the records Bobby's dad kept of Bobby's behavior problem (hitting, kicking or pushing his brothers). As you can see, his dad has figured an average each week, which is the best measure since some weeks contained only 6 observation days.

The lower left-hand side of the graph begins with 0. Bobby's dad has written Bobby's highest *before* score near the top, and has filled in the other numbers on the side. This is the only tricky part of graphing—deciding what the range of numbers will be. The number at the top should be just a little higher than your *before* measure.

Next, Bobby's dad simply transferred his averages onto the graph by making a dot across from the appropriate number and then connecting the dots.

If you like to see your records in graphic form, then you can follow these same simple procedures. But whether or not you make a graph, make sure you keep your daily record chart faithfully.

Trouble-shooting

If your records show that the behavior problem is decreasing, good! If, however, your records over the weeks show little progress, there are a variety of ways you might *troubleshoot* your program. Ask yourself the following questions:

1. Have I correctly identified the *consequence* which is maintaining the problem?

2. Have I really *changed that consequence?* (Or am I still giving the problem some attention, or other reward?)

3. Are other family members also consistently carrying out the program?

4. Am I *encouraging an alternative* behavior?

5. Have I *arranged the antecedents* so that the behavior is less likely to occur in the first place?

6. Have I overlooked a medical problem that might be contributing to the behavior problem (e.g., hearing problem, eye problem, toothache).

Summary

You are now ready to begin a program to reduce your child's behavior problem, using the following six steps:

1. Specify the behavior.

2. Measure the behavior: *Before.*

3. Identify the A-B-C pattern.

4. Change consequences.

   Locate a better consequence.

   Encourage alternative behaviors.

5. Change antecedents.

6. Continue to measure the behavior: *After.*

A final word: Behavior problem management is the most challenging teaching you will do. You may, therefore, find it helpful in the early stages to re-read all or certain parts of this manual and to discuss your strategy with other family members. Once you have come up with an approach that seems sensible, stay with it. . . and good luck!

David's Story: A Review

"Mom. . . David's up there again."

Having just heard the books falling to the floor, Mrs. McKay really didn't need Judy's signal; she was already on her way to the familiar living room scene. And there was David, playfully toppling over everything that stood in his way as he climbed to the top of the shelves. He loved being up there and hardly seemed to notice the damage his adventures caused.

"Get down from there this minute," ordered Mrs. McKay and before waiting for David to respond she went over and dragged him off. "I told you not to climb up there anymore, didn't I?" But David simply smiled as he walked out of the room, looking forward, no doubt, to the time of his next adventure.

That evening, after David went to bed, Mr. and Mrs. McKay and Judy discussed ways they might begin to work on the climbing problem. "He's doing it more and more, it seems," said Mrs. McKay; "not listening to me, climbing on the bookshelves, breaking things on his way up. . . it's terribly frustrating when he does that. Of course, neither of you are home as much as I am, so you don't see it as often, but believe me, it's got to stop."

"OK. You're talking about his climbing, right?" Mr. McKay asked. "Let's leave it at that for the moment, and forget that he sometimes doesn't listen. Now, how many times would you say he climbs on the shelves?"

"The other night when I was babysitting for him, he went up there 6 times. I counted," said Judy. "He was really having a ball."

"That's about right," said Mrs. McKay. "Sometimes it seems that whenever you turn your back on him, there he goes. . . all day. . . maybe as many as 10 times."

"All right then. Just so we can be sure, why don't we keep track—like Judy did the other night—of every time David climbs on the shelves. It shouldn't be too hard since he doesn't seem to worry about giving himself away. We'll just do what we always do when he goes up there, only now, before we do, we'll remember to jot down each time on this chart. . ." and Mr. McKay tore the *before* chart out of the manual.

At the end of one week, the McKay's faithfully kept chart looked like this:

Week (Write in date)	Days							Average
	S	M	T	W	T	F	S	
Week 1	5	9	6	8	7	4	Not home	6½

"Well, it looks like you were both right," said Mr. McKay. "The chart shows that David, in fact, climbed a total of 39 times for the week, not counting Saturday when we all went to Grandma's. That comes out to be 6½ times a day. He's quite a climber all right."

"So what do we do now?" asked Judy. "Are you going to punish him or something when he does it?"

"I think that David might enjoy climbing just because he looks forward to the way I race in after him," answered Mrs. McKay. "I'm sure he gets a big kick out of all that extra attention."

"Makes sense to me," said Mr. McKay. "It sounds like if we didn't make such a fuss over his being up there, he'd give up climbing soon enough."

In a few minutes a strategy for ignoring David's climbing behavior was agreed upon. "As you suggested, I'll take most of the things off the shelves—but I'll guarantee you it won't be easy to keep from running in after him. I just hope it works; but I suppose we'll find out soon enough."

Mrs. McKay was right. At times ignoring became almost impossible, especially for Judy who was always excited by her brother's adventures. But they did it, and at the end of two weeks their *after* records looked like this:

	S	M	T	W	T	F	S	Average
Week 1	No record	6	4	4	7	5	4	5
Week 2	6	7	7	4	7	3	5	5½

"Now what? For two weeks we try as hard as we can not to give any attention to David's climbing, and now look at him—he's climbing just about as many times now as he was then. And of course he's up there longer because we don't make him get down." Mrs. McKay clearly sounded as though she were giving up. "You know, to tell the truth I never really thought it would work anyway. But I'm glad we at least kept the records to prove it."

"To prove what, Mom?" asked Judy.

"Oh. . . to prove that there are some things that children like David will just always do, I suppose. Or at least that there's nothing we can do to stop him. And we certainly tried as hard as anyone could."

"But we were wrong, that's all," said Mr. McKay. "That's no reason to stop trying. Look at it this way: We took away what we thought was the most rewarding consequence to David's climbing behavior—our attention—and he kept on climbing anyway. That just shows we were wrong. . . and that he must be doing it for some other reason."

"I just think that he does it because he likes doing it," said Judy. "Like I said before, whenever I've seen him climb up there, it looks like he's having a ball."

"So then how do you stop making it fun for him?" asked Mrs. McKay.

They talked for quite awhile until Mrs. McKay finally answered her own question: "Whenever we catch him climbing on the shelves, we march him sternly to his room and make him stay put for 3 minutes, is that it?"

"That's it all right."

But not quite. The McKays were now certainly on the right track, but had neglected the fact that David didn't really mind being in his room at all. Indeed, the first time Mr. McKay went to bring him out of Time Out he found David playing happily with his toy soldiers. "He didn't even want to come out. If we're going to make climbing on the shelves have unpleasant consequences for him, then we'd better pick a less happy place for Time Out."

It took time for the McKays to work out a successful program for reducing David's climbing behavior; certainly longer than the two weeks they originally planned. But were you to look in on them today, you'd find Mrs. McKay's candlesticks back up on the shelves where they had always belonged. The many adjustments they had to make, the way they had to continually re-think their strategy and work together as a team finally paid off. Their consistent effort was well rewarded.

And as for David, he'll probably develop some new problem behaviors now and then; what child doesn't? But if you were to go and visit him today, you'd most likely find him playing in the backyard on the ladder that his father built.

TaKe a BreaK!

CHAPTER 4

SELF-STIMULATING and FeARFUL BEHAVIORS

Some children behave in ways which look quite different from the behavior problems we've described so far, ways which do not seem to fit an A-B-C pattern. They might sit for long periods of time, twirling a dish on the floor, continually waving their arms in front of their faces, or casually masturbating. They may seem interested in little else around them. Some might spend much of their time rocking or making funny noises or perhaps pulling at their hair. And, too, there are some children who seem overly afraid—sometimes of many things, sometimes of only one or two. Their fear in these cases is usually excessive, preventing them from participating in much that the world has to offer.

Both of these kinds of behavior—the repetitious, seemingly purposeless ones as well as the fearful ones—fit our description of behavior problems. Yet, often, parents do not see them as such. Many parents we know, for instance, say, ''That's just the way he is.''

Perhaps you tended to accept these behaviors because attempts to change them have been difficult. Even parents trained in the techniques of behavior modification—who have demonstrated their ability to teach children—admit to being less certain about what to do with these behaviors. Their reasons are usually quite correct. As they have told us, with these two kinds of behavior, it is much more difficult to identify the A-B-C pattern. And, by not being able to specify either the Antecedents or the Consequences (or sometimes both), even the best teachers are often confused.

The case where Antecedents are absent or unclear is less common and, in fact, if we look a bit further, there usually are identifiable conditions when the behavior typically occurs. It sometimes helps to ask: When does the behavior not occur? It's also important to remember that Antecedents are not all outside the child; his thoughts and feelings are Antecedents, too.

This makes identifying Antecedents more difficult, of course, because we cannot really know what he's thinking or feeling, but certainly you already know there are some behaviors more likely to occur "when he's tired," or "when he's hungry," or "when he's excited."

It is more often the case that we cannot identify consistent Consequences which are rewarding the behavior. Again, however, Consequences do not have to be outside the child. The feeling of pride and accomplishment at putting together a puzzle cannot be seen but, nevertheless, might be rewarding to him and may maintain his interest in puzzles. We will be concerned in this chapter with those behaviors for which the Consequences are not immediately clear.

Self-Stimulating Behaviors

It is late afternoon, and Mike sits in his favorite living room chair rocking from side to side. There is no one else in the room and Mike's rocking continues uninterrupted for a full half-hour.

If we begin an A-B-C analysis of Mike's behavior, we get partway and then get stuck:

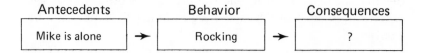

Antecedents		Behavior		Consequences
Mike is alone	→	Rocking	→	?

Mike's behavior does not seem to be maintained by adult attention; it is not helping him to avoid a learning situation. . . just what does maintain it? What *is* the rewarding consequence?

There may be consequences which we simply cannot see. First, rocking is *self-stimulating;* it brings physical sensations which some children evidently find pleasant. Other repetitive behaviors such as headbanging, flapping arms, twirling an object in the sunlight, hitting ears, banging objects together, and the like also bring sensations. Second, the child with limited skills is in an environment which offers little opportunity for play or, if he does not know how to participate in whatever opportunities do exist, he cannot find rewards in the ways most children do. Attempting to participate, in fact, will often lead to failure, and these attempts will soon be abandoned.

It may be that by performing any one of these simple self-stimulating behaviors a child can ignore the changing demands of the world around him and rest assured that in his own unique way he's establishing a strategy for knowing what to expect. We've often heard references to children being "in a world of their own" when they engage in such activity. By learning to control this world of their own—even if only for short periods of time—many children find at least one way of dealing with ours.

Thus, although we cannot see them, the *rewards* of self-stimulating behaviors might be:

The physical sensation itself

Predictability and sense of mastery

And, since we cannot change the reward itself—the Consequence—our best approach for modifying self-stimulating behaviors is to concentrate on:

Encouraging alternative behaviors

As the child learns to play with toys, to interact with other children, to enjoy watching television, to sing songs and so forth, his self-stimulating behavior will decrease because:

1. These activities are usually incompatible with self-stimulation.

2. These activities, once mastered, can bring greater rewards than the physical sensations of self-stimulation.

With the child who engages in repetitive, self-stimulating behaviors, the best modification technique is to teach her play skills so that she can fill more of her day with enjoyable activity. Remember, too, that we are considering self-stimulating behavior to be a problem and, as such, you should deal with it as described earlier. Most important, you should never reward it with attention of any kind. For, while self-stimulation often begins when the child is alone, your attention later on might help to keep it going longer (as though the child were saying to herself: "If I keep this up long enough, someone's bound to notice me"). You would, of course, always be wiser to give lots of attention only when the child is not engaged in self-stimulating behavior.

Mark screams angrily, bites down hard on his already scarred hand and slams his head against the wall. His little brother quickly tries to give Mark back the toy, but it's too late.

Self-Abusive Behaviors

When self-stimulating behaviors can inflict actual physical damage on the child, they are called *self-abusive*. They are not often as continued as self-stimulating behaviors, but are quite a bit more terrifying. They are dramatic, unpleasant to see, and most significantly, they hurt—both the child who may cause permanent injury to himself and the parents who are left to wonder why it happens and what they can do about it.

Self-abusive behaviors are the most difficult of all to modify. First, as with the milder forms of self-stimulating behavior, it is difficult to specify the A-B-C pattern. Sometimes, as when Mark's brother took away the toy, the Antecedents are clear and involve a kind of provocation. But for other self-abusive behaviors, the Antecedents are not so clear. Headbanging, pulling out hair, hitting the eyes or ears, digging at an arm or leg—often we are left to question what could possibly have led up to these behaviors.

So, too, with the Consequences of self-abusive behaviors. Typically, they attract quick and varied attention. Also, like the milder forms of self-stimulation, self-abuse provides a physical sensation. Finally, such behaviors often get desired results since those around the child often must rush to end it, and cannot think objectively in terms of the consequences of their giving in to these strong demands.

For all of these reasons, self-abusive behavior is perhaps best managed from a preventive point of view. Since most children with these behaviors become especially self-abusive when frustrated, teased or angered, you must learn to recognize the warning signs and be prepared to "nip any outburst in the bud" before it has a chance to become full-blown. Often this will mean rearranging antecedents; it will also mean teaching the child more useful skills and other ways to express frustration and anger.

One last reason for the difficulty in managing self-abusive behavior is the general lack of professional understanding of these problems. As a result, any suggestions we might offer must be tentative at this point, and certainly incomplete. And yet there are guidelines you can follow: The most important of these is to give whatever approach you choose enough time to prove itself, one way or another.

Look first for a possible A-B-C pattern. Does the self-abusive behavior help the child to get her own way somehow? How do you react to it? Do you become upset, yell at her, rush in to prevent her from hurting herself? Do you usually give in to her demands, or stop teaching her, or try to soothe her? It's pretty difficult to avoid any of these responses; it's almost impossible to be a parent and casually ignore such behavior. Yet it is possible that your reaction in part maintains her self-abuse, and you must look very carefully at your behavior to see if this is the case.

If you are going to give your attention to self-abusive behavior, then it should be in the form of strong punishment.

This, too, is not pleasant for you, but it is about the only way to be effective. You know best what she likes least! A very loud "No," a hard slap on the hand, physically restraining her for a short period, putting her in her room for Time Out are all possible punishments and each has proven effective in reducing some children's self-abusive behavior. The punishment should be given *immediately following the beginning of the self-abusive behavior, every time she does it.* And you should be sure to keep a careful record of the behavior so that you can see if your approach is succeeding. If over time the self-abusive behavior is decreasing, then you have found an effective punishment. If the behavior remains unchanged, or increases, your punishment is ineffective and may even be rewarding from your child's point of view.

Finally, you should be sure to withhold all possible rewards from her whenever she is self-abusive. Difficult as this may be, you must try to be consistent in not giving pleasant consequences to this behavior. Make sure, in general, that the behavior in no way "pays off" for your child.

An additional note

Some self-stimulating or even self-abusive behaviors can become quite habitual; the child does them without really even realizing it. Such behaviors may be seen even in the verbal child who has many skills and, in fact, even the child of normal intelligence is apt to suck her thumb, pull at her hair, bite her nails or perhaps rock, often without being aware of what she's doing. For children who have better communication skills, it is sometimes effective merely to remind the child whenever she is doing something inappropriate. Especially for the child who wants to be rid of the behavior—and wants your approval—such reminders can be quite helpful to her. On the other hand, if any kind of attention from you is rewarding, this approach will backfire and the behavior will increase. Again, the only way to know is to keep accurate records.

Reminders which make the child more aware of the behavior can be paired with rewards for getting through a given period of time without producing the behavior.

Of course, you would start with very short periods and make them progressively longer as the child gains more control over the behavior and it decreases.

Reminders and rewards may be effective with the verbal child who has a good repertoire of skills. With the nonverbal or minimally skilled child, the chances are that he will not understand the plan and will simply respond to your attention.

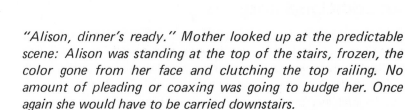

example Sammy's mother was helping him to become more aware of his habitual thumb-sucking.

"You can watch TV as long as you don't suck your thumb."

Every time the thumb went in the mouth, the favorite TV program went off—and remained off until the thumb came out again.

It was only a short time before Sammy could watch a whole TV show without any thumb-sucking at all. And when he became *more aware of his behavior*, he could be quietly reminded of it in other situations as well.

"Alison, dinner's ready." Mother looked up at the predictable scene: Alison was standing at the top of the stairs, frozen, the color gone from her face and clutching the top railing. No amount of pleading or coaxing was going to budge her. Once again she would have to be carried downstairs.

Fears Everyone has fears of some kind: Fear of heights, fear of the dark, fear of animals, fear of speaking in public, fear of thunderstorms, fear of hospitals. . . the list of fears a person might have is endless.

Fear can be very helpful when it serves to protect us from a real danger. We learn to stay away from objects or situations which could harm us. We learn to cross the street carefully, to be careful around fires, to keep our hands out of the lion's cage at the zoo, and so forth. Over time our fears come to be replaced by a sensible amount of caution.

However, fear can be a problem as well as a help. If our fear is too great, we devote too much effort to worrying about when the next dog or thunderstorm or nightfall is coming and to arranging our life to avoid fearful situations. Our fears can thus become a burden to us. We might never learn to deal with these feared situations successfully since we typically go out of our way to avoid them altogether. And so the fear continues.

For children, fears can be a particularly big problem because they are less free to plan their lives so as to avoid fearful situations. They will more frequently confront the cause of their fear and struggle to escape or avoid it.

Fears do not really follow the A-B-C pattern we have described in this manual. As you may know from your own experience, the feeling of your heart pounding, your palms sweating, and the sinking feeling in your stomach are not maintained by pleasant consequences—you would be happy to be rid of these feelings. In fact, feeling fearful often has unpleasant consequences. It is likely, therefore, that fears are learned in a different way from the other behaviors we have discussed and so they must be changed in a different way as well.

First it is very important to know whether your child's behavior means she is afraid. Alison is asked to come down stairs, yet she stays at the top of the stairs. We must consider at least three possible explanations:

1. Alison *does not know how* to walk down stairs (she needs to be taught this skill).

2. Alison *gets pleasant consequences* for refusing to obey (her behavior problem is being rewarded and maintained by pleading and coaxing).

3. Alison *is afraid.*

It is usually possible for a parent to know if the child is afraid; you come to know what signs to look for—clinging, getting pale, crying and the like. In some cases you may even know the history behind your child's fear of certain objects or situations. It is hardly unusual, for example, for a child who has been in a car accident to continue being afraid of cars. Or if a child was once scratched by an overly playful kitten he may have developed a long-lasting fear of cats.

If the child is afraid, our approach to changing behavior will be different from the one we have discussed so far. Consider the following example:

A father reported that, after moving into their new house, his daughter trembled and cried every night when she was put to bed, something she had never done before they moved. Not wanting to "reward" this new behavior, he ignored it, and it became progressively worse. He wanted to know why.

The reason may well have been that his daughter, in fact, was *afraid in her new situation.* She was not, in other words, crying to get attention; indeed she hadn't ever needed to before. So, by ignoring her quite natural fears, the father in this instance made her all the more afraid and all the less able to control her crying.

Before making any decisions about how to alter this behavior, it is important to ask yourself if the child is acting frightened for any of the following reasons:

1. She lacks the skills.

2. She is receiving pleasant consequences for behaving in this way.

3. She is afraid, and has no control over how she is behaving.

If the behavior is identified as *fear,* then your approach to reducing it will resemble the gradual teaching of a skill.

Strategies for reducing fears follow closely from the principles of skill teaching. Let us review these principles here:

1. Choosing a goal

2. Breaking down the fear into small steps

3. Proceeding gradually

4. Rewarding appropriate behavior

If we can teach a child not to exhibit those behaviors which we immediately recognize as "fearful behaviors" in whatever situation typically frightens him, then we must assume he is no longer afraid of that situation. Thus, in the simplest sense, the goal of any fear-reduction approach is to decrease the exhibition of fearful behavior. At the same time, the approach teaches the child skills for participating in those situations which previously frightened him. As with all behavior problems, then, the goal is to encourage alternative, more adaptive behaviors to replace fearful ones.

Any fearful situation can be broken down into smaller, less frightening ones. Take a child, for example, who is afraid of dogs. The most terrifying situation for him might be to have a German Shepherd jump up on him. But we can easily imagine other dog-related situations which would be less frightening: Looking at storybook pictures of dogs, for example, or seeing a dog in a movie. In between these two extremes we can also think of a number of situations involving dogs that range from mildly to very frightening. (Note, for example, the list on page 65.)

An important step in reducing a fear is to make up a list of situations as we did with fear of dogs above. This involves imagination and sensitivity on your part and should be given careful thought before the final list is written down. And the list definitely should be written down! Don't hesitate to ask for help when developing your list; see if other family members agree about which situations are more and less frightening to your child.

Obviously there is never only one correct list for any given fear. You will, therefore, have to take a close look at the important dimensions *of your child's fear situations* and build these gradually into a list designed specifically for him. In the following example, the list tells us that the fear varied on dimensions such as whether the child was inside or out, whether the dog was leashed or free, and whether the dog was little or big.

Least 1. Seeing a picture of a dog in a storybook.

2. Seeing a dog in a movie or on TV.

3. Looking out of the window and seeing a dog in the yard.

4. Being outside and seeing a dog being walked across the street on a leash.

5. Being outside and seeing a little dog in the next yard running free.

6. Being outside and having a little dog approach.

7. Being outside and patting a little dog.

Most 8. Being outside and having a big dog jump up on him.

For Alison's fear of walking down stairs, the important dimensions were how many stairs she had to walk down and how much support was available. The list for her fear might have looked like this:

Least 1. Walking up stairs (which is no problem).

2. Walking down the one step at the front door.

3. Walking down the three steps in a play staircase.

4. Walking down the last three steps of the staircase at home, holding mother's hand.

5. Walking down the last five steps of the staircase, holding mother's hand.

6. Walking down the last seven steps of the staircase, holding mother's hand.

7. Walking down the last three steps of the staircase, holding the banister, with mother's verbal encouragement.

8. Walking down the last five steps of the staircase, holding the banister, with mother's verbal encouragement.

9. Walking down the entire staircase, holding the banister, with mother's verbal encouragement.

Most 10. Walking down the staircase, holding the banister, with mother not present.

4

7

66

If your child has a fear, think of a situation which would be *most* frightening to her and a situation in the same area which would be *least* frightening to her. Write these on the lines below, marked most and least.

Next, think about the various situations in which her fear might occur, and how frightened you think she might become in each. You will, as we've said, need to determine the important dimensions of her fear. Fill in the rest of the list with situations from least to most fearful, varying the dimensions you find to be important.

Least _____

_____

_____

_____

_____

_____

_____

_____

_____

_____

Most _____

To begin helping your child overcome his fear, you will repeatedly expose him to the *least* fearful situation on your list. As your child becomes comfortable in this situation, and exhibits no fear, you will move to the next step. You will continue to practice each step until he can be in that situation with no fear.

Also, you will want to assure that he is not very afraid when you practice these situations. One way is to proceed very gradually. However, it also helps if you can create in your child another feeling—like excitement, security, happiness, which is *incompatible* with anxiety. For example, a child is less apt to feel afraid in the following situations.

1. Eating. Gradually expose him to the feared situation while giving him his favorite food.

   Fear of Cats
   While Tom sat at the table eating ice cream, mother sat across the room holding the feared kitten.

2. Doing something pleasant. Sing a song, play a favorite game.

   Fear of Water
   Dad and Jerry began playing about 10 feet away from the edge of the ocean, making a big sand castle. Jerry was having fun and was becoming used to the water being not too far away. Soon Dad would move them a few feet closer, all as part of the game.

3. Imagining something pleasant or exciting. Talk to him about his favorite things, TV shows or people. Tell an exciting story about his favorite story characters, with him in it.

   Fear of Darkness
   "OK, Tommy. I'll be Batman and you be Robin. Wait here for a minute with the light out while I go in the next room and get your invisible ray gun."

4. Feeling physically secure. Stay close, hold her hand, make physical contact.

   Fear of Crowds
   Mother walked briefly with Larue along the busy sidewalk, holding her tightly by the hand.

The food, games or contact will bring about feelings in the child which are incompatible with being afraid. To overcome his fear, then, you will progressively expose him to situations higher on your list while at the same time creating pleasant feelings to assure he is not feeling afraid.

Never force him; but encourage and praise his efforts. Practice a step several times for perhaps 5 minutes a day. You may spend quite a few days on each step. The important rule is to proceed gradually, not moving to a new step until the child is comfortable with the last one.

Notice how this approach resembles the approach of teaching a new skill, and to your child, mastering a fearful situation may feel very much like new learning altogether. We have reviewed several important points in teaching a skill: Choosing a goal, proceeding gradually in a step-by-step manner and rewarding success. There are two other points which also apply: "Setting the stage" and "Modeling."

Setting the stage

As in skill teaching, arrange the situation to be minimally distracting and easy to manage. Try to make sure that your teaching will be as uninterrupted as possible so that there will be no intrusions to upset your child. Keep your directions simple. When teaching Alison, for example, the rest of the family should be warned to stay away from the stairs while she is being taught, and Alison should be on the side of the stairs with the banister.

Modeling

Each feared step is more easily mastered if the child sees someone else master that step first. It is best if the model is another child, so this is a natural place for your other children to help with the program. It can almost be made into a game. For example, when working on an early step in Alison's program, her mother might have Alison's brother walk down the last three stairs, slowly; mother would then praise and reward him. Next would be her *sister's* turn, and finally it would be Alison's turn. If Alison held back and did not want to try, she would not be forced; rather, they might repeat the sequence, making the demand slightly easier by beginning from the next to last stair.

Summary

Below is a brief summary of the points in helping your child to overcome a fear.

1. Make sure that the behavior is in fact a fear.

2. Make a list of related situations in which the child is afraid, ranging from the least frightening to the most frightening. If your child is afraid of several very different things—dogs and darkness—you will need to make several lists and work first on just one of them.

3. Begin with the least frightening item. Set the stage for success and model what you want your child to do.

4. Make sure that he does not become very frightened in this situation by bringing about a feeling *incompatible* with fear.

5. Stay with the same situation until your child can master it with no fear at all; then move to the next.

6. Continue gradually in this way until your child can master all of the situations on your list.

69

example Since Billy slipped and fell in the bathtub, he has violently refused to take a bath, struggling to escape and trembling even when near the tub. Billy's older brother decided to tackle the problem, and first made up a brief list.

Least 1. Being in the bathroom with someone.

2. Sitting next to the tub, playing with boats in one inch of water.

3. Sitting in the bathtub, playing with toy car, no water.

4. Sitting in the bathtub, one inch of water, playing with a boat.

5. Sitting in the bathtub, no water, being washed off.

6. Sitting in bathtub, two inches of water, being bathed.

Most 7. Sitting in full tub, being bathed.

Next, he looked for something Billy enjoyed. Since Billy liked to play with small toys, his brother thought of a clever plan. He bought an easy-to-construct plastic boat and sat with Billy for several evenings on the bathroom rug making the boat. Now it was time to launch it, and putting less than an inch of water in the tub, he made a game of the launching with Billy. Over the following nights he proceeded to higher steps on the list, using the boat games to keep Billy preoccupied and happy as he very gradually became friends with the bathtub again.

response form

Dear Reader,

Most books are written to be read and put away. Now that you've read this one, however, you know it isn't like most books. Rather, our intent is for this material to be worked with continually, both by you and by us.

As you begin to apply the techniques you've learned here, we too are beginning to think about ways to revise this manual, to make it more useful to others like yourself. And so, as we have done with so many parents and colleagues in the early stages of this manual's development, we now ask for your help in this revision.

We would like to send you a questionnaire on which you can indicate specific reactions you had to this manual as well as information concerning how you and your child progressed as a result of using it. Rest assured that whatever you might tell us will be kept strictly confidential.

If you are willing to help us in this effort, please fill out the form below and send it to us. We'll get back to you right away. (You can use this page as a mailer; just cut on the dotted line and fold so that the address on the reverse side shows.)

We look forward to hearing from you and, in anticipation of your cooperation, we thank you very much.

Name: _____

Address: _____

_____

_____

☐ Parent   ☐ Professional _____
                                            (specify)

Are you using this manual: ☐ with professional supervision; ☐ with no professional supervision;   ☐ to conduct parent training;   ☐ other_____
                                            (specify)

Which manual(s) do you have: ☐ Early Self-Help Skills ☐ Intermediate Self-Help Skills   ☐ Advanced Self-Help Skills ☐ Behavior Problems

-------------------------------- (fold here) --------------------------------

-------------------------------- (fold here) --------------------------------

_____

_____

_____

RETURN TO:

Dr. Bruce L. Baker
Department of Psychology
Franz Hall
U.C.L.A.
Los Angeles, California 90024

Behavior chart

What exact behavior are you observing? _____

When are you observing it? _____ all day. _____ minutes per day, from _____ to _____

Are you charting _____ how often it occurs   or   _____ how long it lasts?

Chart

Week (Write in date)	Days							Average
	S	M	T	W	T	F	S	
Week 1								
Week 2								
Week 3								
Week 4								
Week 5								

BEFORE   AFTER

Graph

8						
7						
6						
5						
4						
3						
2						
1						
0						

Week 1   Week 2   Week 3   Week 4   Week 5